Enjoy the read
Don Pickerman

DON PECKHAM
REMEMBERS

Newfoundland's unique
humour – Anecdotes

Donald Peckham

Order this book online at www.trafford.com
or email orders@trafford.com

Most Trafford titles are also available at major online book retailers.

Print information available on the last page.

ISBN: 978-1-6987-0525-5 (sc)
ISBN: 978-1-6987-0523-1 (hc)
ISBN: 978-1-6987-0524-8 (e)

Trafford rev. 01/14/2021

www.trafford.com
North America & international
toll-free: 844-688-6899 (USA & Canada)
fax: 812 355 4082

CONTENTS

Fifty years traveling throughout Newfoundland and Labrador, and thirty-five years as a bureaucrat in the provincial government:

- Newfoundland's unique humor
- Anecdotes
- Government ministers: good, bad, and indifferent.

Don Peckham in his Municipal Affairs Office 1994

Dedicated to my father, Fred Peckham, whom unfortunately I didn't get to know well enough. He worked hard at more than one job to look after our large family of ten.

I would like to thank Christine Hawkins and Graham Manual for their work in editing and proofing and their encouragement to complete this work.

INTRODUCTION

I was born on Bell Island during the Second World War. My parents had settled there to take advantage of the prosperous activity from the Bell Island iron ore mines. My father and his brother Orlando had opened a brewery and retail soft-drink plant around 1938. It burned down in 1940, and unfortunately, it was not insured. Instead of rebuilding, the brothers moved back to St. John's, and my father obtained employment at the American Air Force Base at Pleasantville.

From two years old, I grew up on St. Clare Avenue in the west end of St. John's. I grew up in a family not rich in money but rich in love for one another. I went to school at Curtis Academy where I attended from kindergarten to high school graduation. It was a good school with excellent teachers; however, there was a culture that if you weren't scholarly or from a notable family, the teachers didn't pay much attention to you as an individual. There was no counseling for what you were going to do after school and never did anyone suggest to me that I could possibly attend university, so I never thought of that as an option. The school later was burned down.

After graduation, I got work at the Great Eastern Oil Company office on Water Street as an office boy. Every Friday, I would walk from the store on Water Street to the nearby bank with a leather satchel and pick up cash for the payroll for the entire company and return walking up the street with it. You probably wouldn't do that today! After a short apprenticeship there, I realized there was not much opportunity for promotion, so I moved on to work with the Newfoundland government starting in the Department of Education.

While working, I took courses at Memorial University and completed certifications in both business administration and public administration. In addition, I affiliated with the International Association of Chartered Secretaries and Administrators where I was awarded the designation Public Administrator and later was honored with the designation Fellow Chartered Secretaries and Administrators.

I worked for the Newfoundland government and/or Crown Agencies for over thirty-five years, and during that time, I traveled to every nook and cranny in Newfoundland and Labrador. Many times in less than ideal weather conditions and sometimes driving or flying in very dubious conditions to make a deadline. Some of these will become clear in the following stories.

I did have what I later called missed opportunities. While I was working in the Expropriations Division of the Department of Public Works and Services, I became acquainted with many of the local solicitors and their law firms. One day, a prominent lawyer, who later became a judge, came to see me and offered to fund me to attend law school to seek a law degree. I discussed this with my wife, and she was not in favor as we had two small children and she was not prepared to make the sacrifice that would be needed while I was attending university.

Some years later, with the children grown up, I was recommended by the Department of National Defence to be the first civilian Newfoundlander selected to attend the Department of National Defence Executive training program. This would be a nine-month assignment with all expenses paid. The program was held in Ottawa with tours in most of the NATO countries, visiting their governments and learning from them. At the end of the training, you would be granted a certificate in international business equivalent to a master's degree in business.

I had discussed this with my wife, and she knew how excited I was to have such an opportunity. Unfortunately, I did not know that she did not like the idea, and she went to my deputy minister and advised him that I could not go for various reasons and my acceptance was cancelled by the government before I knew that this had happened. I guess such is life!

All the stories are based on events in which I was directly involved over the years. They are not intended to make fun of any individual or incident but rather to express the natural humor found in things that happen in our everyday lives and hopefully allow us to laugh at ourselves. In some cases, I have used actual names, and in others, I have used fictional names, as I did not want to offend or embarrass any person or their family.

I have drawn from my experiences of traveling the province over a period of thirty-five years, often staying in less than five-star accommodations, but always with five-star hospitality and usually with lots of humor and mostly good food. In addition, I have been involved in the Sea Cadet organization since I was eleven years old. I am still involved in promoting the Navy League Cadet and Sea Cadet youth training organizations through my volunteer activity with the Navy League of Canada. In addition, I have also drawn on my growing up experience in a west end neighborhood of St. John's. There were many unique and sometimes amusing incidents over that period.

I would like to start by acknowledging three of my former bosses for their role in furthering my business knowledge and practices. These were people that I admired, and I modeled much of my development on their practices. Neither would realize the positive impact they had on my life, but I am eternally grateful to them, and I would like to thank them.

The first one was George Warren, physically a giant of a man. His face was weather worn, which made him look tough, and this, combined with his large size, intimidated some people and made them keep their distance. But I knew him as being very smart, having a gentle heart, and he was one of the fairest minded people that I knew. He was knowledgeable in an extensive array of topics and would challenge you on any proposal, but he would listen to reason and support you if he was convinced that you had a good proposal. He would often say "Show me a person that makes no mistakes, and I will show you a person that does no work." He willingly shared his knowledge and provided positive direction on any issue that he knew you were interested in or any project you had taken on.

I had found the true person through my daily dealings with him. He had a great sense of humor, and he would stand behind my decision if for some reason it was later challenged. In the world of politics, many decisions were challenged and not always for economic or good planning reasons, but sometimes to meet the political needs of the government of the day. I learned from George the art of compromise, to listen to people, and to be fair to all people; and as we were working in government, he taught me the need to be fair to members of all political parties whether they were in government or in the opposition, and I did this throughout my entire career as a senior bureaucrat. He was indeed a great positive mentor.

The second boss, Albert Vivian, was also a bright person with a great deal of knowledge in the housing business, but he was unable to make a decision until there was a crisis situation. I dubbed my training under his management as MBC (managing by crisis). When I discovered this trait in him, I would simply deal with my assignments, resolve the issue, and then advise the chairman that it had been done. He was always grateful, and I think he was happy because he did not have to make the decision. Apart from that, he was a person of great character and had high ethical standards. He always tested our recommendations, and he would analyze our proposals carefully and challenge our reasoning before accepting them.

The third gentleman, Tom Whalen, also was a little rough but had a heart of gold, and he was a no-nonsense, get-the-job-done person. He was an intelligent person, a professional engineer, very able to read others, and had a knack for finding solutions that would be agreeable to all parties involved. We got along well, and he taught me many things. I always remembered a quote that I still use when advising younger business professionals, which is "There is a fine line between stupidity and principal." He taught me this once on an issue that I was wrestling with, and after I considered all the factors, I decided to soften my principle and accept a compromised solution. His dedication, sense of humor, vast experience, and unwavering support was invaluable in shaping my business approach.

In addition, I would also like to thank my wife, Elizabeth, for encouraging me to record and share these experiences, incidents, and humor. She has been a tower of strength to me, very encouraging of my activities and supportive in my many pursuits. For that I thank her.

CHAPTER 1
GROS MORNE NATIONAL PARK DEVELOPMENT

While my stories are drawn from my whole life's experiences covering several different phases, I have chosen to start with stories from my days working in the Gros Morne National Park. In the midseventies, I was the coordinator for the development of the newly created Gros Morne National Park. This was one of the most exciting, challenging, and rewarding jobs I ever had.

It was during this period that I noticed and payed attention to the uniqueness of the Newfoundland and Labrador distinct culture and our unique sayings. We have an ability to look at things differently to better deal with the realities of our rugged geography, our isolation, and the ever-changing climatic conditions.

The Resettlement Program/Burn
Some Government Buildings

As the coordinator for the development of the National Park, I was given the authority to research policy and recommend to

1

the government how to proceed to acquire the homes in the five communities that had to be relocated and to recommend which services needed to be upgraded in the enclave communities in order for them to obtain the maximum benefit from this great new developing tourism opportunity. In preparing for this, I reached out to other areas where national parks had been developed, and in some of the readings, I discovered that the governments of several provinces and the government of Canada were having great difficulty with residents of some of the national parks that they had developed. Many were discontented that they were not given enough compensation to acquire an alternate home to replace the one taken for the park development, and they became very discontented.

I arranged to meet with government representatives of several provinces and representatives of some of the citizens committees in these areas. In New Brunswick, I believe the community representative we met with thought I was a representative of homeowners, and he freely offered me advice. He said that the only way the governments would listen to his residents was when they burned down a few bridges, churches, or other community property. He offered to come to Newfoundland to "lend us a hand" should we ever have the need to burn some buildings. Needless to say, I merely thanked him for his offer and used the advice as lesson in how not to proceed.

The relocation policy the government agreed on was very sensitive to individual and family needs and was totally voluntary. It provided an opportunity for families to trade their home, which often were too small and in need of repairs and upgrading. They could choose to either have a new house constructed or to take the equivalent value in cash and construct or purchase another home themselves.

We had learned of the problems in other national park relocation programs where sometimes people would agree to take the cash and spend it on other than housing and then be left without any means to relocate. To avoid this, we would advance cash on a progress basis as various phases of the new home was completed, or we would pay the money in trust to a law firm when other properties were being purchased. This worked very well, and the end result was that most residents ended up with an improved home than the one they previously had.

Well, over 90 percent of the residents chose to take advantage of the relocation policy. They mostly moved into newly constructed homes in nearby communities still within the Gros Morne National Park area.

When owners were selecting their homes to be built, they were allowed a new home size based on the number of bedrooms in their present home combined with the size of their family. If the home only had two bedrooms but there were four children, they would be entitled to a three-bedroom home, etc. They also had a choice of plans to choose from, and they could choose their own color schemes.

When it came to selecting a plan for one family, they advised me that they knew exactly what they wanted. They wanted the house exactly like the one I lived in. That met the criteria as it was a standard three-bedroom bungalow that was within their entitlement. When the house was built, and it was time to select the interior colors, they advised me that they didn't want any of the old pastel colors that I had on my walls. They wanted a bit of color. They picked out mustard yellow for one bedroom, dark purple for another, and orange for the third bedroom. For the kitchen, living room, and hall, they selected a bright pea green. The finished home was very colorful indeed.

Moving Houses

As part of the program of purchasing properties, when we acquired a home that was in reasonably good shape, we would look at the possibility of moving the home to another community and turn it over to the Department of Welfare, as it was then called. They would use it to house clients that were in need of accommodations.

We moved about twenty or more houses over time, and sometimes moving them presented their own unique challenges.

One such case was a house acquired in Belldown's Point. After checking it out, we were satisfied that it could be relocated and reused.

There would be an additional challenge in moving this house as it was a little larger than any we had moved before, and it had to be brought across the St. Paul's Bridge. This bridge is a different structure than most local bridges in that it has a superstructure built above and over the bridge.

I had our construction crew check to see if the home would fit through the bridge structure. It was measured and then the spacing through the bridge was checked. We found a problem. The bridge has inside rails about four feet high, and the house could not fit between these railings.

However, if we lifted the house above the level of the rails, it could fit through but with only inches to spare. I needed a Department of Transportation and Works permit to haul such a wide load along the main Northern Peninsula Highway. I checked with the regional superintendent in Deer Lake, and he refused to issue the permit as he was concerned we might not get the house through the St. Paul's Bridge. I had advised him that I was confident we could get it through and, in addition, should there be a problem, I would have a tractor present and a crew with chain saws. We would cut part of the house off if it became stuck on the bridge. At most, this would only delay traffic for fifteen to twenty minutes.

He was still not satisfied and would not issue the permit. I was determined that this house was too good not to be reused for a family that otherwise would be without adequate housing. Therefore, I called my colleague Lou White, the deputy minister of the Department of Transportation and Works in St. John's, and appealed to him to have the permit issued.

With my assurances to have a crew and equipment on standby in the event the worst thing happened and we could not get through the bridge, he authorized the issuance of a permit with the safety concerns addressed and written into the permit.

That was great, and the next day, we bought in a low-bed transport truck and had the house loaded onto it but raised on supports so it would be high enough to clear the inside railings on the bridge. This made for a precarious load, and the truck could only proceed at a very slow speed along the highway.

To think that our challenges with this house were over was an understatement. Firstly, as we commenced to pass through the bridge, the house occasionally would scrape along the top of the inside railings, and there was a danger it might become lodged on the rails. We had not factored in that the bridge would move slightly with such a heavy load or that the level of the rails was not always even.

We could not raise the level of the house on the flatbed any higher as there were only inches of clearance from the roof of the house to the inside structure of the bridge. When we got about halfway across the bridge, the eve of the house touched the bridge structure, and we were afraid to proceed as it might hook in and dislodge the house from its supports on the truck.

Our emergency crew were immediately put into action and cut off a small section of the eve to allow enough room to continue to cross the bridge. The driver then continued to gingerly creep along the remainder of the bridge and finally made it through without further incident.

However, there were more challenges ahead. There were some twenty-five to thirty telephone lines across the road going through Sally's Cove. Earlier, houses that were moved could fit under them without incident, and a few times, we would lift the lines with a long pole to allow the house to fit under them.

Because this house had been raised on the flatbed some four feet, it could not fit under many of these lines. This presented a dilemma. We had a large load on the highway that had to be moved off without undue delay as we could not tie up the traffic any longer than absolutely necessary.

The proper thing to do was to contact the phone company representative in Corner Brook and have them send up a crew that would drop the lines to let us pass through. This would take a considerable time, possibly a week or more, so it was dismissed as a viable alternative.

I decided to tell the driver to navigate the truck on through and break the lines, and I would discuss this with the phone company after we arrived safely with the load to its new location in Rocky Harbour.

We proceeded along the way and had to break some fifteen to twenty phone lines. I did have our superintendent check each line to make sure they were not power lines, and we were lucky none of them were. There was one power line crossing, but it was high enough that it was not a concern for us.

When our house arrived at Rocky Harbour, I contacted the phone company and told them of the problem and explained the circumstances and the reason for the decision to break them. He was not happy but did agree to immediately dispatch a crew to reattach them, which he did the same day.

When the house was set up again in its new location, the family that was assigned to it was more than grateful to be placed in such a comfortable housing unit.

I was happy that the risk and the extra work of getting it there was well worth the effort.

The Money Guys

Staff in our Gros Morne office became known the money guys, as we were taking inventory of who owned land that we had to purchase for the park development. While driving around, we quickly noticed fences being installed where there never were fences before. The "owners" were staking out their territory so they could claim a share of the compensation.

One day while driving through one of the enclave communities, I noticed a guy cutting pointed tops of long posts and stacking them. A week or so later, driving through the same area, I noticed the guy planting the posts in the ground with the pointed end on top. He apparently saw his neighbors cutting and pointing posts, and he did the same thing, except he failed to notice that the posts had pointed ends so they could be driven into the ground. He had dug holes and planted, fence posts pointing end up around some two acres of land.

Property Valuations

In order to establish fair market value for each of the private properties, their fishing gear, etc. that was stored on it we hired a professional property appraisal firm to contact each owner and conduct an assessment.

After the assessments were done and I had received the valuation reports, my assistant Reuben Harding and I began to contact the owners and offer them the appraised price for their property. Initially, they would all tell us that we had the property undervalued and that they owned a lot more land and other assets than what was described in the report.

I called the appraiser and went over some of the reports with him to ensure that he had not missed any information, following which he assured me that he kept meticulous notes and had included all that the owners had advised him they owned.

I returned to some of the owners to further question them, and during the conversation with one of them, it became clear that the owners had mistakenly thought that our appraiser was a tax assessor and they were minimizing the value of their property and assets.

I explained to them that our appraiser was not associated with the taxation people and we needed to be aware of their full holdings in order to properly compensate them for it.

I had to have our appraiser revisit all the owners and reassess what they owned. Following that, we did not have any problem negotiating reasonable settlements with the property owners.

They almost did themselves in hiding their full holdings thinking they were reporting to the taxation people.

Threatened by a Newfoundland Ranger

One day Reuben Harding and I visited an elderly gentleman whom I shall call Samuel (not his real name) in one of the communities to be relocated. After what I thought was an amicable discussion, he went into the next room and came out with a .303 military rifle. He proceeded to tell me that he was a member of the Canadian Forces Rangers and their job was to protect the land and if I had any intention of forcing him to move out of his home, he would use it on me. I advised him that I had no such intention, but rather was here to advise him of the options available to him should he decide he wanted to relocate any time. He assured me he had no intention of moving until he was in a "box." We parted thinking there was no way this gentleman was going to relocate.

A few months later, my secretary came into my Gros Morne office to tell me that Samuel was in the reception area and wanted to see me. I told her to bring him in, and as he sat in front of my desk, I was curious to know what he wanted. He told me that he had decided to take our offer to build him a new house in one of the enclave communities. He said that all his children had moved, the community store had closed, and there was no purpose for him to stay there by himself.

After his house was built and he moved into it, he once again came to the office and asked to see me. He came in and sat in front of my desk and took a flask out of his pocket and said, "Young man, I want to offer you a drink," as he was so happy with his new home and the fact he was still in the area with his sons and other relatives. It was very heartwarming and a great relief to know that he obviously had changed his mind about having to use the .303 gun on me.

My Own Fence

We built several subdivisions and offered the homes to families that agreed to relocate from park communities. This was a good program and enabled us to complete the relocation of five full communities without any major trouble. The property would contain a new house and be completely fenced. One day, I went to visit a few of the relocated families to see how they were adjusting. I noticed that one of them, Mellissa and Sam Parker, had installed a new fence on both sides of the property parallel to the fence that had already been installed.

Mellissa and Sam were an older couple who kept to themselves but had lots of pride in what they owned. They tried to maintain it to the extent they could afford. I am not sure if Sam ever worked, but he was always in the woods cutting wood for the stove or for fencing. And he would snare rabbits as food for the family. He maintained a small vegetable garden in his backyard to supplement their food.

I knocked on their door and was welcomed in by Mellissa. We had a little chat about the weather and things, and when Sam joined us, I questioned him why he built a new fence immediately inside the fence we had installed between the two properties. Sam stated that fence belonged to his neighbor, as it had been there before he was, and he wanted to have his own, so he cut the logs over time up in the country and erected one a mere two inches inside the other fence. This was indeed a funny sight.

The Furnace Doesn't Work

After Sam and Mellissa moved into their new home, Mellissa was continuously calling and complaining that her furnace was not working properly. At first, I would have my staff call the local merchant who installed the furnace and have him check it and fix the problem.

However, the calls continued over a period of time, and the merchant would check the furnace and advise me it was working properly. So when the next call came from Mellissa, I decided to go to the home myself to see what the problem was with the furnace.

When Mellissa opened the door and invited me in, I was nearly floored by the blast of heat. I asked her what seemed to be the problem, and she advised me the furnace works sometimes and then it goes off and won't come on until she turns the little dial on the wall up. I had a look at the thermostat, and it was set to 90 degrees. I turned it back to 72, explained that it was normal for the furnace to cut in and out, and advised her not to turn it up anymore. I tried to explain the process of how the furnace is different than the woodstove she previously had in that it did not stay on all the time. I knew she was not understanding the rationale, so I decided I needed to use something dramatic to convince her. I took a chance and told her that if she turned it up any higher, the furnace might explode. She said, "Oh, I don't want that to happen," and I never received any complaints about her furnace after that.

The Mayor Did All That in One Day—Wow

I had a planned trip to St. John's from Deer Lake on a King Air airplane, and as there were spare seats on board, I invited Robert Blythe, the mayor of a small community, along for a visit to St. John's. The mayor was excited, and I advised him of the time to meet me at Deer Lake for our flight to St. John's. The weather was fine, and it would be a good evening for flying.

We met at Deer Lake Airport, and the King Air plane was there waiting. We took off on time, and when we were airborne, I decided to mix a drink and offered the mayor one, which he gladly accepted. We spent the hour-long flight talking about the Gros Morne development plans and the possibilities for his community to take advantage of the tourism opportunities that would be available.

On arrival in St. John's, I took him to Holiday Inn and checked him in there and advised him that I would be back later in the evening to take him out to dinner. I picked him up about seven thirty and went to a Chinese restaurant for dinner. He seemed to enjoy his dinner, following which I brought him back to his hotel and advised him I would pick him up the next day to take him to the airport for our return trip home.

I went to the hotel to get him in the morning. It was a beautiful fall day, and the flight should be smooth and enjoyable. After we got airborne and settled in with a drink, I asked him how he enjoyed his visit. Robert said that it blew his mind. He had never been on an airplane before, and he flew in a private plane and even had a social drink on board; he had never been in St. John's before, never stayed in a hotel before, and never had Chinese food before, and "I did all this on one trip." He was just amazed that it was possible to do so many new things in one or two days.

Buying a Casket

When I first moved to Rocky Harbour, I soon got accustomed to going to the local grocery store to buy all sorts of things. It was more than a grocery store, as it sold all sorts of hardware, fishing supplies, and clothing as well as groceries. But I never thought that would be where you would go to buy a casket.

One cold blistering winter morning, my wife asked me to take her to the store to pick up some items for the weekend. I braved the elements, and we drove down Main Street to the local store. We were in the process of picking out some meat when we heard a commotion at the main door. When I looked, there were a couple of guys covered in snow looking agitated, and they were carrying in another person. They said they were from another community across the harbour and had braved the wild weather to drive around the bay, so I guessed they must have needed something urgently.

They spoke to the clerk and told him that they wanted to buy a coffin for Uncle Bill, and as he was a very tall guy, they brought the corpse over in the back of their truck so they could make sure they got a casket to fit. Of course, the store owner suggested they bring the body back out to their truck, measure the length of the body, and come back; and he would make sure he gave them one that was long enough for their departed friend. They did this, and the clerk took them into a back room, and in a few minutes, they returned carrying a casket.

They went outside and placed Uncle Bill into it to make sure it was a proper fit, and when they were satisfied, they returned to pay for it and then left to return home around the other side of the bay.

My wife was a bit skeptical about buying her meat in the store after that experience.

It wasn't until my next visit to the store that I saw a sign hanging over the inside of the main door that read "Coffins sold here." It was only then that I realized that in a remote area, the local merchant was counted on to provide all the essentials to support the resident's needs. This was truly a full variety store.

Unique Hotel Key

Gros Morne National Park is large, some 750 square miles; and on one trip, as I had a lot of owners to see in the northern end of the park, I decided to stay in a nearby local hotel in Cow Head for the night. When I checked in, the clerk handed me a kitchen knife. I advised her I was not going to dinner yet, and she said, "No, the knife is used to open your hotel room door as we do not have any keys." So I went around with a kitchen knife sticking out of my topcoat pocket for the two days. I didn't think there was much privacy, as the knife could be used to open any hotel room door.

Car into a Snowbank

Weather conditions often played a role while working in the Gros Morne National Park. However, we learned to work and deal with the weather no matter how bad it was, and this was especially true in the wintertime. The Gros Morne area seemed to have its own microclimate, and you could not count on the weather forecast from Corner Brook to judge what it might be like in the Rocky Harbour, Trout River, and Cow Head areas.

My colleague Reuben Harding and I would always just look out the office door and determine if it was suitable to go on the road or not. Even this didn't mean very much, as we might leave Rocky Harbour in fine weather in the morning and be caught in a raging blizzard somewhere later in the afternoon. This happened all too often.

Our office was in Rocky Harbour, and on one bright sunny but very frosty winter day, we had an appointment to meet some people in Trout River. We judged the weather to be suitable and left the office around ten in the morning to drive around the northwest arm of Bonne Bay to Woody Point and onward to Trout River.

The road from Rocky Harbour to Woody Point was reasonable, mostly covered with snow with icy patches periodically, but not too difficult to drive on. However, the road from Woody Point to Trout River was not as good as it had been, covered in packed snow that had slightly melted with the bright sunshine, making it very slippery.

I was proceeding along at a reasonable speed, a bit slower than usual, due to the slippery conditions. I was chatting away with the other people in my car and turned my head for a moment, and when I looked forward, I was on a sharp turn in the road just above the community of Trout River. I often admired the view from here in the summertime, but not today. I quickly turned the steering wheel, but the car refused to respond; instead, it kept going straight directly toward a steep drop-off into a valley below.

I tried braking, but that didn't work, as the sun had melted the snow, and it became frozen into a clear sheet of ice. After a few seconds, I knew that I could not keep the car on the road, and I told everybody to hang on as we were going over the embankment into the snow below.

The car slipped to the edge of the road and continued down about sixty to eighty feet and landed upright in about ten or more feet of snow. The car was buried up to our windows. A quick check with my passengers confirmed that they were all OK except for the good scare we all had.

We got out through the car door windows and climbed up to the road. We waited for someone to come along, and when a pickup truck came by, the driver agreed to drive me to Woody Point so I could get someone to go get my car.

That was no easy feat. The local tow truck in the area was usually the fuel oil delivery truck, which normally was used to pull cars out of snowbanks. But there was no way the oil truck was going to pull my car up from an eighty-foot ravine over trees and shrubs and tons of snow.

I thought for a moment and felt that the only thing that could get my car back on the road would be one of the Department of Transportation tractors. So I went to the highways depot and told the foreman of my dilemma. He said that he was going to have a grader on that road later in the afternoon, and he would ask the operator to see if he could pull my car to the road.

I had lunch at the local motel in Trout River, and when I was advised that the grader was on the road, I got a ride back to my car and waited for the driver to arrive.

The operator looked at where the car was and said he didn't think he would be able to pull it from its location, but he would try at my risk. We tied ropes and chains together to get enough length to reach the car, then walked down the side of the hill through the ten-foot-deep snow to get to the car. It was a hard job digging in the snow to get at the front of the car to get the tow rope on, but after a while, we managed to get it hooked up.

We climbed back up the bank to the road, and the tractor operator began to slowly drive up the road to pull the car from its landing point. It was slow going, and the car was being tossed and tipped as it was pulled toward the road over the trees and bushes, but luckily it remained upright.

It took about ten minutes or so to get the car to the road, but the operator was very skilled and managed to get it completely back on the road. I surveyed the car, and there did not appear to be any damages, so I thanked the operator, and we got into the car, and drove back around the Bay to our office in Rocky Harbour, none the worse for the wear.

It was not uncommon for cars to slip off the road in the area in the wintertime, and when one did, everybody that came along would stop to help, and usually within a few minutes, the car would be back on the road and on its way again. This particular time was an exception as my car had left the road in an area where there was a big drop-off, and I was lucky that a grader was able to pull it up to the road.

Ploughing into a Snowdrift

On another occasion Reuben Harding, my assistant, and I left Rocky Harbour to go to St. Paul's in the northern end of the park to meet with some residents. It was a fine winter day, lots of snow around but none falling, and the sun was shining. We drove to St. Paul's and had our meetings and were ready to return home by four o'clock in the afternoon. By then, the wind had come up, and it was snowing briskly. This caused whiteouts and large snowdrifts across the road in a number of areas.

As I came to each drift, I normally could see beyond it, and if there was no traffic coming in the opposite direction, I would drive the car, hoping to get through the drift. However, I wasn't too far south of Sally's Cove when I encountered a drift larger than the others. The wind was blowing harder, and it became almost impossible to see where I was driving. There was no way to see if anything was approaching from the opposite direction.

I stopped by the enormous drift, thought about it a bit, and then decided the chance of meeting another oncoming vehicle was remote because of the stormy weather, so I could take a chance to see if I could make it through this drift.

I backed my car up so that I could get a good run at it and headed directly into the drift holding onto the steering wheel as tight as I could, and I hoped against hope that I could make it safely to the other end of it.

As I entered the drift, there was a large *woof* and sudden total darkness, and the car stopped. We were stuck somewhere in the snowdrift. I tried to open the car door and several of the windows, only to find out we were totally buried in snow.

Reuben tunneled his way out using his hands and then kicked snow away from my door enough to get it open so I could get out. We climbed to the top of the snowbank and walked to the end of the drift some thirty or so feet to the roadway.

We both said we were glad to be out of the car as we knew that there was a large truck somewhere behind us, and we were afraid that he might try to do the same thing to get through the drift, and he would surely crash into our car. We were on the wrong side of the drift to warn the truck driver, so we agreed that I would stay at this end of the drift to warn any cars going north, and Reuben would go to the other end to warn any that came from the north going south.

Before he could get to the end of the drift, we heard a loud thunder and saw a truck with snow flying everywhere coming out the other end of the drift. He did not see my car and luckily somehow missed it. The driver saw us on the road and stopped to offer help. He told us that he had passed a snow plough just a short distance back coming this way, and he would likely clear the area, so we could get the car through.

Reuben quickly scampered to the northern end of the drift and waited for the plough to arrive. We were luckily well-dressed and could withstand the blistering cold wind and the snow blowing in our face. When the snow plough arrived, the driver began clearing the drift until he exposed my car. He cleared the snow around it, and we were able to once again proceed on home.

While working in the Gros Morne Park was lots of fun and very challenging, it also had it tough moments such as these times, but we just continued on and coped as best we could with the uncertain weather conditions.

The Mummers

In 1972, we were to have the official ribbon cutting ceremony to announce the formal signing of an agreement between the government of Canada and the government of Newfoundland to jointly develop the Gros Morne National Park. Honorable Ed Maynard was the provincial government minister responsible for the park development. He was also a member of the House of Assembly for the area, and Honorable Jean Chretien was minister of Northern and Indian Affairs (later to become prime minister) and the federal minister responsible for the park development.

I had arranged an outdoor ceremony in a local field, and all the nearby community residents were invited to this memorable occasion. Well, it turned out to be even more memorable than we had planned. The ceremony was set for 2:00 p.m., and in the morning, I had arranged to take the two ministers on a boat tour of Northwest Arm to see the spectacular views of the Table Mountain, Gros Morne Mountain, and the surrounding villages. While on the tour, I received a radio message advising me that there appeared to be trouble brewing at the official opening site. A group called the Mummers had arrived and were coaching and encouraging the residents to protest the park development when the ministers arrived.

We decided to proceed with the ceremony, and when we arrived at the site, the protesters had dug a ditch across the entrance way so we could not enter by car. We got out of our vehicles and proceeded to walk to the opening platform, and once there, the crowd, urged on by the Mummers, surrounded the platform that we were on and chanted protests. They would not let the ministers make their announcements without interruption and loud shouts. However, the ministers proceeded and cut the ribbon. But when we were ready to leave, we were hemmed in by protestors and could not move from the area.

There were too many people for us to safely try to escape forcefully, and there were only two Mounties in the area. They would not be able to contain the crowds if anything were to happen. We decided to wait it out until RCMP reinforcements were bought in from Corner Brook over an hour's drive away. When they finally arrived, they made a small escape route, and we were able to squeeze our way to the safety of our cars. We went to the local hotel and continued with the planned reception for invited dignitaries and guests.

I was not sure what the group were protesting as they had never consulted us on any of our policies or programs. The relocation program as it turned out went extremely well. It was well received by the residents involved, and I did not receive any negative feedback from the local communities.

My Fall from Grace

When I went to Rocky Harbour to live during the Gros Morne development, I soon discovered how long the winters can be, and I learned that I needed to participate in winter activities with the local guys to learn how to enjoy the snow activities. Nearly all the locals had several Ski-Doos, and I decided that I should get at least one, which I did. It was a brand-new machine, and I tried it out a few times and discovered how much fun it was to operate, and I soon became a pro at it. Every Saturday, a group of friends would take an expedition over the Long Range Mountains on their Ski-Doos, and they invited me to come along. I was excited to get to see the country this way and packed all my gear, met up with the group at the local service station, and we all departed through the country.

It was a great cold but sunny and clear winter day, and the snow was crisp underneath the skis of the Ski-Doo. We would stop occasionally to admire the scenery and boil the kettle for a warm mug of tea. When lunchtime arrived, we decided to try our luck at catching a few trout through the ice. One of the guys had an auger and began to drill a hole while another set up his fishing pole and baited his line.

We managed to catch just two trout and decided to put them on the pan over the open fire and fry them for lunch. They were delicious, and we shared the balance of our food and had a winter picnic. There is nothing better than a picnic in the country even in the wintertime.

The group were plotting where they would be by suppertime. I had not realized they were going for a full day and evening and did not bring enough spare gas to make such a long trip. Therefore, I advised the group that I would head back immediately after lunch, which I did.

It was a magnificent clear, sunny winter day. I had no trouble finding my way over the well-worn trail, and when I arrived back in Rocky Harbour, I remembered there was an area where there was a slope down the side of the hill to the frozen harbor from where I could shortcut back to my house. I was traveling along the cliff, looking for the access to the Harbour, when suddenly my Ski-Doo began to slip sideways toward the edge of the cliff, which was about sixty-five feet high. I tried to steer clear of the danger, but the machine would not respond, so I cut the engine and got off but held onto the machine, hoping to stop it, but to no avail. The machine continued to slide sideways to the cliff edge, and when I was at the point of no return, I pushed the machine as hard as I could so it would not fall on top of me as we tumbled down the rocky cliff.

I was not wearing a helmet or very good Ski-Doo clothing, but luckily, I did have a pair of well-padded Ski-Doo mitts on. As I started to tumble down the cliffside, I had enough presence of mind to put my hands in front of my face for protection from the sharp protruding rocks. When I hit the ice and looked up, my machine was still pounding its way down head over heels, banging hard off the rocks until it finally hit the harbour ice upside down. After a few minutes, I was able to get my breath back. I checked to see if I had any broken bones and discovered that I was still able to walk. Everything seemed to be all right, except for the pain in every part of my body. I checked the machine to find that it had compressed itself to about half its original size, and it was obvious that it was no longer able to run. I then limped the mile or so back to my home. My two gloves were shredded, but they did a marvellous job of protecting my face.

After a week or so, I gradually recovered from my many bruises and then got the courage to purchase another Ski-Doo. I quickly learned how to properly drive it and how to stay out of danger. I continued to enjoy many expeditions over the Long Range Mountains with the boys, and I always went prepared with spare parts, gas, and food.

No Support from My Own Government

During the Gros Morne development, one of the main functions was to acquire all the land for the national park. So over time, we became known as the money guys as we purchased all the 750 square miles of property. The majority of it was Crown land, but there were a few thousand private holdings.

It was traditional for people to own land simply by occupying it for a long period of time. There would not be any legal title, but sometimes the property was occupied by several generations. We would have the "owners" obtain affidavits of long-term possession, which we would recognize as valid title. There was soon a flurry of fencing around tracks of land, some of which was used and occupied for a long time, and others that the owners wanted to claim they had for a long time in order to get paid for it.

In such a closely-knit area, neighbors were always curious to know what each other was paid for their property, as they wanted to be sure they were fairly compensated in relation to what others received for their land and buildings. However, there were always rumors of greatly inflated payments being made to some individuals.

I advised all our office staff of the need for discretion and that all negotiations with owners were to be kept in the strictest of confidence and could not be divulged by staff. Over time, there were rumors circulating in the community, and this was obviously creating some discontent. It became clear that someone on staff was providing detailed information to residents on the value paid for various properties without providing the reasons for the differences. I called the staff together and advised them about my concern and reinforced the need for confidentially, but it continued. I eventually learned that Sally, our office clerk, was the staff member that was telling neighbors what various people were receiving for their property.

Residents would get upset when they heard that one of their neighbors who had a house and garden received more compensation than they did as they also had a house and garden. They did not consider that there was a difference in the size of the house or garden, which determined its value and whether there were other out buildings or if there was a vegetable garden for which we would provide compensation and there could be other mitigating factors to be considered.

One day at work, Sally, the office clerk, didn't turn up for work and didn't phone in sick as was the normal practice. After a few days, there still was no contact from her. After a week of absence, one of my other assistants came in to see me and advised that he knew why Sally didn't turn up for work. He was sitting in the local hospital waiting room and met Sally there. She advised him that she had a new baby and that she had fooled Mr. Peckham as she was able to work right up to the day before the baby was born, and he didn't know about it.

After several weeks with no contact from Sally, I decided to advertise and fill the vacant position, as it appeared that Sally didn't intend to return to work. I notified her that as she had not returned to work nor had she made arrangements to have a leave of absence, the job had been declared vacant.

A few weeks later, the MHA for the area, who was also a minister in the government, and was my boss arrived in my office and wanted to discuss a letter he received from Sally. She told him that "she had to go off work on sick leave and she could not tell him the nature of the illness, but now she has a baby to support and she can't see why Mr. Peckham won't give her back her job." In the meantime, she had not contacted me to discuss whether she could have her job back or not.

I told the honorable minister the story of her being responsible for leaking private information and the fact that she went off work without discussing it to arrange leave nor did she explain her circumstances. He asked me if I might consider her for a position at a later date, which I agreed I would do.

In any event, I had decided from the outset that we would have every parcel of land that we were to acquire appraised by a qualified appraisal firm, and I would base the offer on the actual appraised value. In addition, I would make an allowance for injurious affection to compensate for any disruption caused by the purchase and to cover the cost of relocating their household and personal effects. This could include the fact that the land was used to grow vegetables for the family, and because of the land acquisition, they no longer had property on which they could continue that practice. So an allowance for that would be made and added to the offered price.

Everybody wanted to know what everybody else got for their land so they could be satisfied that nobody got more for the same-sized property than they did. As they compared, they could see that there were value differences, but they didn't know or understand the reason why, and therefore some felt they had been gypped. As the word spread, there were accusations that some residents were given more favorable treatment than others, and they pressured government to look into it.

One of the local businessmen, who also was the local justice of the peace, joined this group and spread the word that the compensation was increased for certain political friends of the government of the day. There was not a shred of truth to any of these allegations, however the pressure continued to grow to the extent that government decided to set up a public inquiry. Judge Cummings of the provincial court was appointed as the chairman of the inquiry, and he hired two high-powered solicitors to assist him. He commenced public hearings and various people appeared and told their story, and his two lawyers would take this information and use it to question me and my staff.

Two noted things happened, which gave me great concern. First, the minister responsible and to whom I reported appeared before the commission and told the chairman that Don Peckham had been hired by government to research policy, recommend to government policy for the property acquisitions, and that government had approved his recommendations. Therefore Mr. Peckham is the best person for you to question about these issues. He shrewdly ducked any responsibility and passed it on the bureaucratic level and directly to me.

The second incident was that during the hearings, the local justice of the peace, Gordon Shears, who was also a prominent businessman, decided to advise the inquiry that I was biased in making compensation decisions that I was politically motivated and paid whatever I wished to friends of mine and the government of the day. He went further and was libeling me and my character greatly in his presentation.

I interrupted the proceedings and asked the judge if he would postpone the hearings so I could engage legal representation since I was not prepared to allow someone to tear my character to shreds with lies and innuendos. The judge was not sympathetic and would not grant a postponement.

Immediately after the day's hearings, I telephoned George MacAulay, the assistant deputy minister of the Department of Justice, who was also the legal representative for the department I worked for, and advised him what had taken place and asked him to send out a government lawyer to represent me at the hearings. When I explained the situation to him, he stated that while he knew me well and could not believe the allegations, he could not provide me with legal representation as if there was any truth to the allegations, he would have to commence prosecution proceedings against me.

I totally felt like I had been completely let down by my employer and was deemed to be guilty without having a chance to have my say. Now knowing that I was on my own, I immediately contacted Clyde Wells, a prominent solicitor (later to become premier) whom I had known slightly through some business dealings, and asked if he would come to the hearings and represent my interest. He stated that he would and that he would be at the hearing the following day. A short time later, he called me back to advise that he could not represent me as he had previously represented the firm of the person that libeled me, and it could be seen as a conflict of interest. However, he had asked one of his colleagues to represent me, and he came to the hearings the next morning.

After a discussion with me, he asked the judge for a postponement of the hearing so we could decide how best to proceed. The judge agreed and granted a week's postponement. My solicitor later attended the hearings with me and was instrumental in not allowing the local justice of the peace to unjustly malign me or my character.

However, in my mind, the local justice of the peace, because of his standing in the community, had cast a shadow on my character and reputation, which would impede my future dealings with some residents and certainly give me a bad name to many of the public.

When the public inquiry was completed, the judge issued a detailed report to government that stated that he did not find any wrongdoing or any cases of unfairness or biasness in any of my dealings with the residents. However, in my mind, it did not do anything to undo the accusations made directly at me by the local justice of the peace.

When the hearings were over, I obtained a copy of the transcript of the proceedings and decided that I was not prepared to have my name libeled without challenging it with a view to clearing it up. I went to a local prominent lawyer Fintan Aylward and sought his advice. He felt that there was no doubt about the liable, and he agreed to represent me if I wished to sue Gordon Shears and seek a public apology.

We did this and won the case. Gordon Shears was convicted and found guilty of libel and slander and was ordered by the judge to publish public apologies in the local *Gros Morne News* and the *Western Star*, which was widely published in the area from Corner Brook. In addition, he had to pay me a settlement for the damage to my character.

Needless to say, I had incurred a considerable legal bill from the two law firms, which I had to pay myself for damage caused me as a result of carrying out my duties as a public servant. I did not appreciate George Macaulay's stand on this and felt that he should have offered me reasonable legal representation, and if found guilty of misconduct, he then could have taken whatever he felt was the correct course of action.

I decided to write the minister to whom I reported and outline what had transpired and advised him that I felt unfairly treated. He agreed and subsequently recommended and received cabinet approval to reimburse me for out-of-pocket legal expenses.

Later on, I was advised that the Department of Justice had stripped Mr. Shears of his justice of the peace authority as he had a criminal conviction against him. I felt that there was some justice as all the residents would know what had happened and why, and I would not be seen in the maligned light that I believed I otherwise might have.

Interesting and unexpected things can happen during an inquiry like this, and this one was no exception. The two lawyers for the inquiry would go through the list of property owners that we dealt with, and in addition, they would respond to complaints made by some residents and grill me in detail as to why a certain amount of compensation was offered. I would always check the property file and show that the property had an independent professional appraisal conducted and the offer was based on that.

However, there was one property that I was questioned about that I could not locate the file, and therefore I could not show what the compensation offer was based on. I kept telling the lawyers, day after day, that I did not have time to check that particular property, and I knew that they were skeptical, thinking something was wrong with the value. Each day they would ask me about that property for a period of two weeks.

One evening, I received a call from Reuben stating that he found the file. It had been accidentally knocked down behind the filing cabinet, and he was lucky enough to have spotted it.

It was a great relief the next day when the lawyer once again asked me if I had a response for this property, and I was able to tell him that, yes, I could table a copy of the appraisal, which was exactly the same value as had been offered to the property owner.

CHAPTER 2
MY FIRST HOME PURCHASE

How Can So Many Things Go Wrong?

This is an interesting story about the trials and tribulations of a first home purchase. It shows how many things can go wrong that one could never anticipate.

In 1962, my brother Fred had bought a building lot in a new subdivision called Wedgewood Park just outside St. John's off Torbay Road. After several years of waiting for its completion so he could commence the construction of his new house, the developers went bankrupt and the project was closed. After a period of time, a new developer, Chester Dawe Limited, took over the subdivision and advised my brother that he could have his building lot when they were ready, but they would not refund his money, which he had initially paid for it. However, by then, Fred had acquired another lot in a different subdivision and constructed a new home. Rather than give away the value of the lot, he offered it to me, which I gratefully accepted.

I was working with the Newfoundland government at the time as a very junior clerk, and the salary was indeed very meager. When I approached the lending agency, Central Mortgage and Housing

Corporation, I was advised that with my level of salary, I would need an additional fifteen hundred dollars as security before they could consider financing the new home construction.

I thought about it for a while and then approached my bank and asked if I could get a loan of fifteen hundred dollars, which they agreed to. I put the money in my bank account and got a letter from them confirming that I indeed had fifteen hundred dollars in the bank and brought it to CMHC. They took my application for financing and, in a few days, advised me it had been approved. This was great news as I could then approach the developer and commence the planning for the construction of my new home.

The following week, I went to the bank and repaid the fifteen-hundred-dollar loan with the same money I had borrowed from them. I was never sure why CMHC wanted me to have this extra money.

In 1964, I contracted Chester Dawe Limited to construct a new home for me with a completion date for September that year. As the summer passed, it became apparent that the developer could not complete the development on time as there were numerous problems with the installation of the water and sewer infrastructure. I and two other families had been promised that the subdivision would be completed and our homes constructed in time for us to move in before Christmas 1964. By late November, our homes were built, but they were not inspected by CMHC for financing, as the installation of the water, sewer, and roads were not completed.

By mid-November, we were getting concerned and started to press the developer, Chester Dawe Limited, for action. They had told us that there were leaks somewhere in the new water system, and they would do their best to find and fix them. A few weeks later, we again contacted the developer and were promised they would have a representative meet us at the site Saturday morning. I and Mrs. Lebans, who also was waiting for her home to be completed, were there bright and early, and a backhoe operator turned up, but no representative of the company came to speak with us or to tell the operator where to dig or what he was to do.

Mrs. Lebans was a very resourceful person, and she instructed the operator to commence digging up the water line to look for the leak. The operator complied and started digging, and after a little while, there was a great clunk as the backhoe had hit the water main and broke the section off. No need to panic, Mrs. Lebans instructed the operator to continue and remove the broken section and replace it with a new section, which he commenced to do. It was a bitterly cold day, and there was a concern that the exposed water main might freeze and add to the problems.

Mrs. Lebans went into her house where she had stored some of her household effects and bought out a fur coat and threw it into the hole in the ground and told the operator to wrap it around the pipe, so it would not freeze.

Around midday, the company representative arrived, and after having a heated argument with me and Mrs. Lebans, he started to supervise the repair work. In the freezing cold weather, the supervisor and excavation operator moved from area to area, digging and repairing. They found some leaks and, over the course of the next two days, had them repaired.

This was great news for us, and we arranged for CMHC to inspect our new homes so they would approve our financing. The next day, I was informed that there was a problem with the foundation of the house, and it did not pass inspection and therefore could not be financed by CMHC or another conventional mortgage company.

As our occupancy date had long since passed and Christmas was now just a week away and with considerable pressure from me and Mrs. Lebans, the company agreed to let me move into one of their model homes while they constructed me another home.

I got the go-ahead to move in on Christmas Eve. I rounded up a few friends and started to move in our few possessions as we wanted to be in our own home for Christmas. It was Christmas Eve, and there were boxes everywhere, but there were no curtains to the windows, no Christmas tree, not even a single Christmas decoration. It looked like we would have to celebrate Christmas day without a Christmas tree or any decorations, but we were prepared to do it as long as we were moved into our own home.

After supper, we decided to have a glass of wine when a knock came on the door. One of my good friends arrived with a Christmas tree that he and his wife had pulled on a sled from Torbay Road, pulling it over the snowbanks that had accumulated on the road. He and his wife installed and decorated the tree. A few other friends arrived and hung curtains and put up a few decorations, and the next day, we enjoyed an exhausted but splendid Christmas day.

I thought the major problems were over, only to find out that we were living in a subdivision during the winter, and there was no snow clearing arranged, and the company was about to declare the subdivision project bankrupt. We eventually arrange for snow clearing by a gentleman who had a farm tractor. On more than one occasion, the snow was too much for his little farm tractor, and he would drive in over it and tow my car out to Torbay Road. Somehow, we survived our first winter there.

I was naturally excited to be getting my first new home, but this was only the beginning of many more challenges dealing with this construction company to get my own house completed and in securing adequate municipal services for the subdivision. It eventually happened, and we were able to move into the new home, and together with the other residents that moved into the subdivision, we set up a local service district to manage the provision of municipal services. A few years later, we changed the status of the community from a local service district to a community council.

Wedgewood Park was a closely knit community, and the residents did not want to give up their identity and merge with the much larger city of St. John's. I was the only person of all the residents that recommended it become a part of the city of St. John's, which it eventually did. This was the sensible thing to do in order to take advantage of the economies of scale in the delivery of water, sewer, fire services, etc.

CHAPTER 3
LOCAL SERVICE DISTRICT OF WEDGEWOOD PARK

Wedgewood Park

This was a new subdivision known as Wedgewood Park and was not well supported by the developer, and municipal services were meager. So eventually, I and a few other residents decided to call a public meeting to discuss the future of the development, and we decided it would be best if we could form some sort of municipal structure.

We formed a committee and approached the Department of Municipal Affairs and requested approval to form a municipality. Eventually, after much persuasion, the department agreed to allow us to form a lower level of municipal governance called a local service district. This gave only enough power to the community to deliver basic municipal services that was sufficient at that time. A few years later, we upgraded the community status to a community council on which I served as the vice chairman, and we were able to deliver a higher level of community and municipal services.

Wedgewood Park was located off Torbay Road on the outskirts of the city of St. John's. We had met with the mayor and city clerk of St. John's to discuss the possibility of us being able to connect into the city sewer services, however the City officials were not interested in helping us. Therefore, we set about on our own to upgrade the sewerage treatment plant to accommodate the growing demand of our expanding development. It was impossible to finance much work, as there were not enough residents to support the large financial expenditure required. So we had to develop a plan to make this work while considering various options available.

Then one day, we were approached by Mr. Craig Dobbin, who wanted to build a new Kmart in St. John's east, but it was denied a permit as the city did not want to jeopardize the new Zellers development that they had recently approved for construction on Torbay Road. Mr. Dobbin found a parcel of land outside St. John's boundary on Torbay Road, but it was within the area of our newly created municipality, Wedgewood Park.

He proposed to develop a new Kmart complex, and Wedgewood Park would become the beneficiaries from the taxes the development would pay. We saw this as a blessing for our new town as we would get a shopping center close by and would receive the business taxes from it. As we did not have full municipal status at the time, we had to get around the problem of not being able to tax this new enterprise.

We approached the Department of Municipal Affairs and asked for their planning assistance and for approval to form a full municipal government. We eventually received approval to become a community council, which gave us the required power to approve commercial establishments and to tax them.

We then entered an agreement in principle with Mr. Dobbin, and he commenced his planning for the new complex. After a few days, I was told that the city of St. John's heard about our intention to grant Mr. Dobbin approval to construct the new Kmart, and they were not happy to see it go ahead so close to the newly approved Zellers complex on Torbay Road. I heard that they were applying pressure to the Department of Municipal Affairs to disband Wedgewood Park and annex the area to St. John's so they could cancel the Kmart proposal.

I called my colleagues on the council and advised them of what I had heard, and we decided to immediately call a council meeting and to issue the approval to Mr. Dobbin for the Kmart project. We did this and, the next day, advised the Department of Municipal Affairs that the project had been issued a building approval and could proceed.

There was no longer any merit in having Wedgewood Park dissolved as a council, as the city would have to honor the building permit that had been issued, therefore this action was not followed by government. The development of the commercial center gave the Wedgewood Park community adequate revenue, coupled with the residential taxes, to maintain a high level of community support services and made it a fully self-sufficient community.

The community became very financially viable, and as it was small, a great camaraderie and sense of community pride developed among the residents. Most people knew everyone else living there. We eventually obtained municipal water from the city of St. John's and developed our own sewage disposal plant to provide high-quality municipal services. We then decided to construct a recreation center with an Olympic-size swimming pool to provide good recreation facilities for the residents.

However, during the 1980s, the government decided to embark on an amalgamation program throughout the province in an effort to reduce the number of non-sustainable communities and form larger ones where there could be efficiencies in their administration and the delivery of municipal services. It was ironic that I became the commissioner for the public hearings for communities on Northeast Avalon, which included Wedgewood Park. It was not surprising that I was the only person of all the residents of Wedgewood Park that recommended it become a part of the city of St. John's, which it eventually did.

CHAPTER 4
SEA CADET EXPERIENCES

Sail Races

It was a lovely summer day at HMCS Acadia in North Sydney, and as a cadet at the age of thirteen years, I was standing at the boathouse with the other one hundred or so Newfoundland cadets marveling at all the buildings and facilities and the hundreds of other cadets from all over Canada.

Then the officer in charge came over and told me that we were going to have whaler races, and as I was the corps leader, I would have to form a team to compete with the other cadets by province. None of the cadets from our St. John's Corps had ever been in a clinker-built whaler before, let alone race in one. However, to maintain our pride, I formed a seven-person sailing crew, and I became its coxswain.

We were given our basic instructions and told to sail out to the buoys, go around them, and return to the wharf to our starting spot.

We raced out of Sydney Harbour, with a lightly blowing wind, weaving around the other ten boats, reached the turning buoy about a mile from the start, and made a fast turn around the marker buoy and raced back to arrive at the wharf in first place.

When we tied the whaler up, the instructor congratulated us on our excellent seamanship and asked if I had raised the drop keel in the boat. I had no idea what a drop keel was, let alone whether I had raised it. He explained to me that it was the board in the center of the boat that was lowered by the rope attached to it to give the boat stability and keep it from capsizing while sailing. Well, I told him it was raised as we didn't know what it was and therefore did not have it lowered during the race. He told me that this likely the reason we won the race, but we were lucky there was not a strong wind blowing as we probably would have all ended in the water with an upside-down boat. Such were the experiences!

Discipline Issues

Sometimes there would be a bully in one of the units who was always creating trouble, and when the officers didn't know who was causing the trouble, we were all punished. The bully would often pick on smaller guys and torment them. A group of us more senior cadets would identify these bullies early into the camp period. We would set up a tribunal, which we called the jury (it was a jungle jury), who would bring, sometimes physically, the offending chap before the jury. He would be given a "trial" at which he was presumed guilty and sentenced to punishment, usually a pusser scrub. The pusser scrub would be to put the offender into the shower, and using a scrubbing brush, the kind our grandmothers used to scrub the hardwood floor with, we would put scrubbing soap on the brush, and with only the cold water on, we would scrub the offender from shoulders to feet. Most of the time, an offender was miraculously cured and did not present a problem for the remainder of the training. In addition to curing this problem, other bullies would take note and would not likely torment the younger cadets for fear of getting the same treatment. The senior officers of the day often asked me how we maintained such good discipline among our group, and I could only tell them that it was by applying firm but fair discipline.

I guess this practice would not be acceptable today, but it was certainly effective back then.

A Lesson to Be Learned

It was an overcast day just after an evening of torrential Nova Scotia rain, and the pug-type gravel was thick and muddy. I was a very junior Sea Cadet officer attending camp at HMCS Acadia in Sydney, Nova Scotia, returning to my barracks from the noon meal at the galley. As I passed by one of the cadet barracks buildings, a senior cadet from one of the mainland provinces threw his navy hat out through the second story window of his barracks and shouted to the young Newfoundland cadet walking by to pick up the hat and bring it in to him. The young cadet, not batting an eyelash and without saying a word, walked over to the hat and put his foot into it and rubbed it into the mud and simply walked away.

The mainland cadet was furious and called me to complain about the cadet walking on his cap in the mud and expected me to discipline the young Newfoundland cadet. I informed the mainland cadet that I didn't see anything and therefore did not know if the Newfoundland cadet had done what he alleged and therefore there was nothing I could do about it. I advised him he should come out and get his hat and be more careful not to drop it out the window in the future. I hope he learned a lesson from this incident.

Mischievous Officers

As a junior officer, we sometimes did mischievous things to occupy our idle time. One night at camp HMCS Acadia in Cornwallis, Nova Scotia, a few Newfoundland buddies and I, with some spare time on our hands, decided to go to the cadet barracks after hours and turn the bed of our compatriot Newfoundlander who was on duty there upside down while he was away from his cabin, making his rounds of the barracks building where the cadets were sleeping.

We made a bit more noise than expected, and an officer nearby came to investigate and caught us red-handed. I don't know who was most surprised, the officer, who happened to be the Roman Catholic priest and discovered the offenders were officers, or us, who didn't know what to tell the priest. Anyway, we explained to him that we were only pulling a prank and asked that he forgive us, as if he were to report us, we would have had some hard explaining to our superior officers. We would be lectured and reminded that we should know better, and if we caught cadets doing this, we would have to discipline them. Luckily, we were forgiven by the priest and not even our buddy found out who had messed up his bedroom, but I know he had his suspicions that we did it.

Dealing with Communist Countries

At age twenty-six, I became the commanding officer of RCSCC Terra Nova Sea Cadet Corps with fourteen other young and energetic officers. There was always friendly competition among corps throughout the province and the nation to be the best and do greater things than all the other units.

We decided, for a display at our upcoming annual inspection, to do something spectacular and came up with the idea to put off a show of international navies. We wanted to dress our cadets in naval uniforms from countries around the world and parade the flags of each of these countries. To do this, we needed to figure out how to get the uniforms and flags from all these countries. We got a list of all the Canadian embassies overseas and all the foreign embassies in Canada, and I wrote to each one explaining what we wanted to do and requesting their support in securing an officer's and a seaman's uniforms and a flag from the country they were serving in or represented.

The response was greater than I had expected, and over the next four months, uniforms, flags and other memorabilia started to arrive in the mail. After six months or so, I received a phone call from the Sea Cadet area officer for Newfoundland, Lieutenant Ted Giannou, who was asking in a very concerned voice what I had been up to. I had no idea what he was talking about and asked him what the problem was. He advised me that he had received numerous calls that day from senior government departments and agencies advising him that I had been corresponding with Communist countries and that Canadian customs had confiscated the goods these countries had sent to me while they commenced an investigation. I was ordered not to pursue any further contact with Communist bloc countries, and I would be advised at a later date what action would be taken against me.

After another month or so, and many interviews, I was able to explain that all I intended to do was to get some uniforms for our display and I had done it through Canadian embassies and foreign embassies in Canada. I was given a stern lecture and told to discontinue any further correspondence with any of the Communist bloc countries. Fortunately for me, a fair number of uniforms and flags had gotten through before the authorities had placed the embargo on these countries.

When it got close to our annual inspection, where we intended to wear these uniforms and carry the flags, I was advised by Lieutenant Giannou, the Sea Cadet area officer, that I had not sought approval for this display; and he said that he was not prepared to give us the authority to wear them nor was he prepared to request approval from any of his superiors.

Therefore, if I proceeded with the display at the annual inspection, I would be doing so without approval and would be subject to further disciplinary action. What a dilemma. I thought about what to do and consulted with my fellow officers, and they all wanted to go ahead with the international display as we planned. I assessed what I thought my discipline could be for such a misdemeanor. The fact that I was not a regular member of the Canadian Forces, I thought the worst discipline that could be applied was they could terminate my appointment as the corps commanding officer. So with the agreement and encouragement of my fellow officers, I decided to take a chance and proceed with the display without authorization from the area cadet office.

I had unofficially told the area cadet officer that I was thinking about proceeding with the display, and he told me that if I did, I would be held solely responsible if the Canadian Navy decided to do something about it.

We proceeded with the international display at the corps annual inspection, and in a drill hall full of parents and friends of the cadets, we dimmed the lights, turned on the special lighting effects, sounded the trumpets, and marched out the cadets in their splendour, wearing uniforms from over twenty-five countries of the world, including a few Communist bloc countries, and carrying the flags of these countries. The inspecting officer, a Royal Canadian Navy captain, looked at the area cadet officer and said that he had never seen anything so impressive and well done in his life, and he turned to me and offered his congratulations. At the end of the parade, the area cadet officer came to me and said he was greatly relieved and that he was impressed with our enthusiasm and having put on such a great show.

At the end of the year, it was a great pleasure for me to be notified by the Navy League of Canada that our corps had been selected as the best in Canada and would receive the national award for it.

A Disobeyed Order

Our Sea Cadet Corps RCSCC Terra Nova occupied a few offices located in the basement of the HMCS Cabot, the local Navy Reserve building at the former United States of America base at Pleasantville. In our offices, we had a few filing cabinets, some old chesterfield chairs, a sofa, a few old desks, some casual chairs, and some other miscellaneous office items on loan from the Canadian Forces Station in St. John's.

One day at my work, I received a phone call from the CFS St. John's Station commander Major Bob Vardy asking me to meet with him. I arranged the meeting for the next day. As I left work to go to the meeting, I was curious and a little concerned as it was very unusual for the station commander to meet directly with a cadet officer. When I arrived there, I was immediately advised that the old wartime furniture that had been on loan to our corps from CFS Supply since 1950 was to be returned, as he no longer wished to be held accountable for it. I argued with him and told him that the furniture was all we had and that we did not have funds to purchase more. If we did, it would have to come from fundraising, which was used to purchase band equipment and to support special activities for the cadets. He was not sympathetic; he told me I was being disobedient and ordered me to arrange to return the furniture. I did nothing about it, and during the next few weeks, I received a number of angry phone calls demanding that I arrange for the return of the furniture. After a few more months passed, I received a call from the station commanding officer giving me an order and a deadline to have the furniture returned or the station would break into our premises and remove it.

I consulted with the chairman of the sponsoring committee, Mr. Eric Perry, and he suggested we visit Dr. Harry Roberts, who had been instrumental in forming the Newfoundland and Labrador division of the Navy League of Canada and the first Sea Cadet Corps, RCSCC Terra Nova (my corps), in Newfoundland in 1950.

We met at Dr. Roberts's office and told him our problem. He immediately telephoned the admiral in Halifax. Dr. Roberts was well-known in the navy as he had been the national president of the Navy League of Canada and had an opportunity to meet with the senior admirals at various conferences and meetings. After a brief conversation, he told me not to worry about having to return the furniture.

A few days later, I received a phone call from the station commander telling me that he had changed his mind on the furniture, and I would not have to return it. I did not let on that I already knew this and thanked him for his change of mind. The furniture is likely still in the corps to this day.

The Sleeping Husband

On a visit to a function at the Sea Cadet Corps in Wabush, Labrador, I was accompanied by a friend of mine who was a colonel in the Canadian Forces who had been invited to be the inspecting officer for the annual inspection. We decided to stay over an extra night and were invited to stay at a remote cabin owned by a local businessman so we could do some ice fishing. The businessman had been known to drink a little too much in his past and had been under pressure from his wife and his doctor to lay off the booze, which he agreed he would do. However, his wife knew that she had to keep an eye on him to make sure he didn't stray. We were probably not good influences as we spent the evening playing cards, telling stories, and having a social or two; and he decided to enjoy his evening "socializing with the guys."

Around 11:00 p.m., we heard a vehicle approaching the cabin, and when the owner looked out, he immediately recognized his truck approaching. He darted toward the bedroom, but hit the lit stove in the kitchen on his way. We managed to grab the stove and keep it from toppling over, which would have been catastrophic. The front door opened, and his wife entered to inquire if everything was going OK. Of course, we told her we were having a great time, but as her husband was not drinking, he had turned in to bed early and was sound asleep. She was delighted that he had gone to bed early, and she soon left for home. Her husband came back into the living room and continued his party with us throughout the night.

The Colonel Tackles the Legion Manager

The following year, again in mid-February, I went to Wabush, Labrador, accompanied by the same colonel and an admiral from the Royal Canadian Navy to conduct the corps annual inspection. Following the inspection, we went to the Royal Canadian Legion for a reception being held in our honor.

The legion manager was showing the admiral some of the artifacts on the walls of the legion, and when the admiral's interest peaked at an old rifle, the manager removed it from the bulkhead (wall) and carelessly showed it off. He was unknowingly pointing the gun toward the admiral when the colonel made a sudden dive at him and knocked him to the floor. Most of us present were taken off guard, not sure what had provoked such an outburst from the normally very controlled colonel. When they got up off the floor, the colonel told the manager he was sorry but advised him that he reacted from instinct when he saw the gun pointing at his admiral.

The Cold Barbeque

After the reception, the local chairman of the sponsoring committee advised me that we were going to attend a barbecue. At first, I thought this was some kind of joke as the temperature outside was minus 44 degrees, and there was about ten feet of snow on the ground. I advised the colonel and the admiral what was planned. The admiral declined, as he had work to do in his hotel room. However, the colonel and I accepted the challenge and went along with the crowd. We arrived at a house with ten-foot snowbanks all around, and I immediately noticed several barbecues with smoke coming from them. At that moment, I knew that we really were going to have a barbecue. After an hour or so inside the warm house, the host advised it was time to start barbecuing the steaks. The local crowd went out to cook their meat, but the host graciously agreed to barbecue mine so I could remain inside.

At the hotel, the admiral and I were sharing a suite, which had a common living room, and when we met in the morning, I apologized to him in case I made any noise getting in around five in the morning. He responded that he did not hear me, as he had been up all night on the telephone dealing with an emergency.

He needed to get back to headquarters to attend to the emergency. The military had arranged for a military airplane to be sent in to pick him up to get him back to Halifax. This was great news for me and the colonel, as we were able to get a ride along with him and get home a day earlier, as we otherwise would have had to wait another day to get a commercial flight home. I got dropped off in Deer Lake where I could catch a flight to St. John's, and the admiral and the colonel continued on to Halifax.

The Butler and Two Navy Spies

On another occasion, my very good friend Admiral Fred Mifflin and I were at Churchill Falls, Labrador, to inspect the Sea Cadet Corps there. As we were the invited guests, we were put up in the magnificent McParland House. The McParland House was constructed by the Rothchilds during the development of the Churchill Falls Hydro Electric development project for their use when they visited the site. The property was absolutely first class and had a cook, a housekeeper, and a butler. We were looked after like royalty. The butler was a most interesting character. He was on loan to the project from Canadian Pacific Hotels and was impeccable at doing his job, but I believe the isolation of a small northern community seemed to have gotten to him, and he was acting in a strange manner.

The company had hosted a reception in our honor, and around eleven o'clock, the sirens rang out in town and all the company personnel present were called out to a fire that had started in the transformer station. There was no point in me and the admiral going to the scene as we would only be in the way, therefore we remained and continued to enjoy the company hospitality. The butler had disappeared for a while but later returned and was still behaving in an unusual manner. It was not until several days later when I arrived back in St. John's and telephoned the chairman of Newfoundland Hydro to thank him for their hospitality that I was told that the butler had had a nervous breakdown and had to be taken from the site and returned to Montreal for treatment.

He told me the story that on the evening of the fire, the butler had called him at his home at two o'clock in the morning to advise him that there was a gigantic fire in town and that it was set by the two navy officers (me and Admiral Mifflin) who were spies and wanted to burn the town down. Luckily, we both personally knew the chairman, and he knew that something was not right with their butler, which was confirmed to him the next day when he was diagnosed with a medical problem, and he was immediately transferred out of the area for medical treatment.

Special South Coast Liquor

An interesting event occurred when I was visiting a south coast town as the inspecting officer for the Sea Cadet Corps annual inspection. After the parade, we were invited to the local Lions Club for a reception. This was a relatively mild affair attended by local dignitaries, which included members of the RCMP, the area judge, the school principal, the mayor, and others. After an hour or so, the RCMP officers left and someone shouted, "Let's get the party on the way!" Apparently, they were waiting for the law enforcement officials to leave so they could bring out some special liquor bought over from nearby St Pierre and Miquelon. I continued to enjoy their hospitality into the early hours of the morning.

Lost Cadets

As a junior officer, I was often selected to be the escort officer for bringing cadets from all across the province to Sea Cadet Camp at Point Edward, North Sydney, and later to HMCS Acadia in the beautiful Annapolis Valley in Nova Scotia.

We would travel by train (the Newfie Bullet) from St. John's to Port Aux Basques, cross the Straits of Bell Isle on the Newfoundland ferry, then travel by bus to North Sydney. Later on, when the camp was transferred to HMCS Cornwallis, we would continue by bus to Halifax and then take a day liner train from Halifax to HMCS Cornwallis. This was quiet a journey, especially when one had the responsibility for some seventy or eighty teenage cadets.

The trip across Newfoundland provided its own challenges as I would have a master list of cadets I had to pick up at various stations along the way. I then had to keep track of them for the forty-eight hours it took to cross the island, then on the Ferry from Port Aux Basques to Sydney.

On one such occasion, I was to pick up some cadets from Bonavista, Catalina, and the Burin Peninsula at the Clarenville train station. When I arrived there, the cadets with their parents were on the platform eagerly awaiting the train. I got off the train with my list to call the roll to make sure that I had everybody, and one young cadet, Roger, a twelve-year-old, came over crying his head off. I asked him what was wrong, and through sobs, he told me that he went into the station to get his ticket and the station agent told him that his name was not on the list, so he could not get a ticket to go on the train.

I checked my master list, which had been issued by Canadian National Railway head office in St. John's, and his name was on my list, so I told him not to worry as I would go into the station and get his ticket. I spoke to the station agent and told her of the problem and advised her that his name was on my master list from her head office, but she said that she still could not issue the ticket until she contacted head office and received confirmation to issue the ticket.

This would take some time to do, and there may not be enough time to have it completed before the train was scheduled to leave in a few minutes. I asked her to hold the train until she got it straightened out, but she advised me she could not do that as it would disrupt the schedule for all other stops. I asked her to hurry up and get the approval when I heard the train porter calling out "All aboard." I knew that this meant the train would be leaving in a few minutes. Then I heard the porter call out "All aboard" once again, and I knew the train would be leaving in one or two minutes.

I needed to do something fast, so I took Roger by the hand and said, "Come on with me, we have to board the train." We immediately boarded the train, and it began to pull out of the station. All the other cadets were happily waving good-bye to their parents, but Roger was still crying. I told him there was no need to cry as he was on the train and on his way to camp. He looked at me and said, "Sir, my bags are still in my father's car at the train station."

Anyway, I comforted him and told him not to worry; we would work it out, and I could get him a new uniform when we arrived in HMCS Cornwallis. When we arrived, I purchased some underwear and a few personal items for him, and a few days later, his bags arrived as his parents had foresight enough to immediately forward them on.

Now as if that was not trying enough, when we arrived in North Sydney en route to Cornwallis in the Annapolis Valley on a fine Sunday afternoon, we were waiting for our busses to arrive to pick us up and bring us to Halifax. After an hour waiting, I knew there was a problem. Here I am on the parking lot of Marine Atlantic with eighty teenage cadets and no bus to pick us up. It was Sunday, so all business and the area cadet office in St. John's were closed, which was responsible for making our transportation arrangements was not open.

After the second hour had passed, I decided to find a local bus company and engage them to come with two busses and bring us to Halifax. I was successful, and eventually the busses arrived. To my delight, we were once more on our way to camp. I advised the bus company to invoice the Sea Cadet area office in St. John's and he would be reimbursed, and he agreed. Some six months after, the company was still trying to get their money and the Sea Cadet area officer stubbornly kept telling him, and me, that I did not have proper authorization to hire the busses; and he therefore could not pay for them. This was totally ridiculous, and I visited his office and told him I was going to have to contact someone higher up the chain in the military to see if I could get this invoice paid. He asked me to hold off, and he would see what he could do, and the very next day, he advised me that he had received approval to pay the bill.

How unlucky could I be to have all these things go wrong on one trip? I am barely twenty-two years old myself with a huge responsibility and trying to keep all these things straight. We had a great time at camp, and then I had to repeat the travel back home. All seemed to go well until we arrived in St. John's. I had, among our cadets, several young boys from Mount Cashel Orphanage that had become cadets. While traveling across the province to the rhythmic sound of the train clacking along the tracks, I carefully checked all meal tickets to make sure all cadets were accounted for. But was I ever to be surprised when I arrived in St. John's. When we arrived in St. John's, the Mount Cashel Orphanage Christian Brothers were at the station, along with all the other parents waiting to pick up their boys.

I assembled all the cadets to count them to make sure they were all accounted for, and lo and behold, I was missing two of the Mount Cashel boys. They simply were not there. When questioned, none of the cadets volunteered any information as to their whereabouts. The brothers were anxious and were pressing me for an answer as to where they were. I did not have an answer. To check the cadets as we crossed the province, they were all given meal tickets, and I would collect them at each meal to make sure all were accounted for, and none had been missing from the last meal count.

I was very worried, as I was responsible for their safe transportation, and they had mysteriously disappeared. We advised the Newfoundland Railway officials, the police and the Sea Cadet Area Office. Needless to say, there was a lot of concern. Could they have fallen or have been pushed from the train as we crossed the province? What a dilemma. I am thinking that I could be in deep trouble, and needless to say, I didn't get much sleep that night.

The next morning, I got a call from the area officer advising me that the police had found the two missing boys and they were unharmed. What a relief. Then I asked where they were. I was told that they were from the Corner Brook area, and when the train stopped there, they decided to get off and go home to their parents. As they knew they could not get permission to do this, they arranged with two other cadets to take their meal tickets and eat two meals each time, so they would be counted and not missed.

My other escort trips were not as eventful as that one, but there was always some episode that would add to the challenge and make it forever memorable. There was never a dull moment escorting seventy or eighty teenaged boys such a long distance.

Lt. Governor's Wife's "Accident"

I would occasionally get the opportunity to travel around the province with various dignitaries. On one occasion, I had the pleasure to accompany the lieutenant governor and his wife to inspect the Sea Cadet Corps in Churchill Falls, Labrador. The weather was beautiful, and the trip up there was pleasant and uneventful. We were hosted by the Churchill Falls Labrador Company (CFLCO) at their lovely McParland House. The house was magnificent and had a great view being located on the banks of the Churchill River.

We inspected the cadets at their parade Saturday evening and were scheduled to leave to return to St. John's 10:00 a.m. Sunday morning on the company-owned Queen Air airplane. The pilot was a very charming chap, and he asked me to make sure the group was on time for the planned departure, as he had to make another run back to Labrador with a maintenance crew when he had delivered us to St. John's. I had advised the lieutenant governor's private secretary Saturday of the planned departure time and the necessity of us being on time to facilitate the tight flying schedule for that day.

My party and I were in the lobby at 9:30 a.m., waiting for His Honor and party to gather with us to be driven to the local airport. At 10:00 a.m., they still had not arrived from their room, and I was getting nervous as I did not like to be holding up the airplane, especially as the company was gracious enough to facilitate our transportation. After a short time, the private secretary to Their Honors arrived and advised me that Their Honors were not yet ready. When I asked him the reason for the delay, he quietly said, "I think they are having a little argument about something."

I advised the pilot that we would be a little late due to Their Honors not being ready. About a half hour later, the private secretary again came to me and advised that His Honor wanted to see me in his room. When I went down there, Her Honor greeted me and advised that as it was such a lovely day, she wanted to have a cocktail before leaving to go home and would like me to join them. I really didn't know what to do except to say yes and try to enjoy a mid-Sunday morning Bloody Mary. I felt terribly bad for such inconsideration to our host, as I knew it was becoming difficult for the plane to fly to St. John's and back to Labrador in time to get the work crew into the transmission line before dark that evening. However, I again advised the pilot, and he remained on standby.

Once we finished our cocktails, Her Honor said, "As it is so late in the day, I think we should have lunch before leaving." I asked the housekeeper to prepare us a light lunch, which she did, and we proceeded to enjoy it. Once finished, I was nervous as to what Her Honor might request next; however, she agreed to finish packing and proceed to the airport.

We boarded the plane about 2:00 p.m. and departed for St. John's. The weather was perfect with clear sunny sky and very light wind. Excellent flying conditions.

After an hour or so in the air, Her Honor advised that she needed to use the washroom. The bathroom on this airplane was built into the rear seat. There was a curtain to pull over when you used the facility. The pilot told Her Honor where it was, and she proceeded into it. After a minute or so, we seemed to hit an air pocket and the airplane took a deep dive. When Her Honor came out of the facility, her dress was considerably wet. She advised that when the plane hit the air pocket, the waste in the toilet splashed completely up over her. I felt sorry for her but also couldn't help but think that she got a little payback for her earlier inconsideration.

When we arrived in St. John's and the party had left the airplane, I thanked the pilot and apologized for the delay in returning. I also casually mentioned the air pocket we hit and said I was surprised as it was such a nice-looking day. He looked at me with a big grin on his face and said, "Don, that wasn't an air pocket. I waited until I thought that Her Honor was comfortably on the 'can' and then put the airplane into the dive to pay her back for all the trouble she has caused me as I now have to try to get back to Labrador much later than the crew needed to be there." We both had a great laugh.

CHAPTER 5
EARNING EXTRA INCOME

Selling Flowers and Peat Moss

In the early 1970s, when I first went to work for government, salaries were very low, and it was difficult to save any money or to buy anything special or go on a vacation. In order to have a little extra money, I was always finding new ways to earn some extra cash. One of my friends, Gerry Holwell, worked at Holland Nurseries, and he told me about an opportunity to deliver flowers on special occasions for the nursery. It was an easy opportunity, so I agreed; and at Easter, Valentine's, and other special occasions, I would become a delivery person. We would load our car with flowers and deliver all day long. We would be paid by the delivery, so there was an incentive to deliver as many as possible.

As there were four or five cars delivering the flowers, I soon figured out that if I started early, I could pick out the deliveries and group them to be all in the east end of St. John's. This would save me time going all over town from end to end with the deliveries. In addition, I would be finished first and be able to make a second and sometimes third load before the others returned from their first trip. This activity usually provided me enough cash for a vacation or to buy something special, like a new set of clothes.

After a few years, we wanted to do something different. We had heard that the nursery had some bad debts that were mounting up, so we came up with an idea to ask the owners of the nursery if we could undertake to collect the bad debts for a percentage of what we collected. The nursery had nothing to lose, as they already considered these as uncollectible accounts, so they accepted our proposal.

We started out by visiting the homes of the people that owed the money. We planned to do this in the evenings, as we knew that many of these people worked and would not be home during the daytime. Usually at the first visit, people would tell us they did not have the cash at that time and we would ask when we should come back for it. This would normally be a Friday, payday for most people. We were very relentless and would be back on Friday, and we could collect a large percentage of the money owed. However, it took a few return calls at some homes, but when the people knew we weren't going away, they would eventually come up with the money. We collected about 90 percent of the bad debts and made a handsome profit for ourselves in doing so. The nursery owners were more than surprised and pleased with the level of collection.

Once that was completed, we had to come up with another plan. We noticed that the nursery was using a lot of white moss for making their floral wreaths. We figured that we could collect up moss free on the barrens and sell it to the nursery cheaper than they were importing it for. We approached the owner with our proposal, and he agreed he would purchase moss from us and pay by the pickup truck load. This sounded like a good deal to me and Gerry, so we agreed. Next weekend, we went to the barrens and commenced to gather up moss. We had no idea how long it would take to fill the back of a pickup truck, but eventually, we did get it full. Happily, we set off for the nursery, and when the owner came out to see what we had, there was only a little over a half a truck load. We did not figure in that the moss would settle as much as it dried and as we drove with it. We ended up only getting paid for a part load. The next weekend, we went to get another load, and we overfilled the truck. When we got back near the nursery, we got out and fluffed the moss up to give it more volume.

This worked, and we got paid for a full load. After that, we learned to fluff the load before delivery each time. The nursery owner told us that he liked what we were doing, as he had good fresh moss all the time, and it was cheaper than what he was previously paying for it. Once again, it was an innovative way to earn a few extra dollars.

CHAPTER 6
ECONOMIC DEVELOPMENT

Move from Your House by Tomorrow

On one occasion, the government agreed to construct a fish plant at Marystown and awarded a contract before acquiring the land. I was called in and told to go to the area and acquire the properties as soon as possible as the West Coast contractor had already begun moving equipment to the area and was expected to immediately begin construction.

This was an interesting job, as for the most part, I had to acquire property with very little lead time. And in order not to delay the project, we would be forced to visit the property owner and advise them that their property was needed for the development and we were expropriating it in order to have title within the statutory ten days from the expropriation. This took away the opportunity to have meaningful negotiations, as most people were offended their property was being forcefully being taken away.

I teamed up with an engineer from the Department of Tourism and Economic Development, and we both left that day for the long drive over the gravel Burin Peninsula highway to Marystown. Upon arriving that evening, we checked into our boardinghouse, as there were no hotels in the area at that time. We immediately went to Mooring Cove, where the plant was to be built, and commenced contacting the homeowners to start negotiations. There were three homes involved. We advised each owner that their property was needed for the development and asked each owner if we could inspect the property to evaluate it and agreed that we would return early the next morning with an offer. Once we inspected all the properties, we retired to our boardinghouse to review our data and decide on the value of the offers to make.

We were staying in a very comfortable boardinghouse and soon discovered that the owner made delicious homemade bread. When it came to mealtime, we discovered that the meals would be very meager. The first meal consisted of cold meat, homemade bread, and a dish of jelly. A plate of bread was put out, and when we each took a slice, the owner came over and removed the plate with the other slices on it. I guess for the low rate we were paying for room and meals, that was all she provided.

As we were staying at the boarding home for a week, we soon learned that we needed to visit the local department store and buy some crackers and cheese to have in our room to supplement the meals we were served.

As we needed the people out of their homes as soon as possible, we decided to double the value of the property and offer it conditionally on the basis that the families would move out within two days. Much to our surprise, all three families agreed to the offer and the condition to vacate. One family that had six or seven children later told me that they sent two children with one set of grandparents, two others with the other grandparents, and several with aunts and uncles. I guess the money made it worthwhile, as they told me later that they were able to buy another better and larger house in Marystown and still had a couple of thousand dollars left over. They were very happy with the deal.

One of the other property owners was a gentleman that lived alone, as I thought, and we visited him to offer to buy his home and land. He advised me that there were only two of them living in the home—he and his horse. Sure enough, when he took me inside to conduct an evaluation, there was the kitchen couch, which the owner slept on, and the rear end of the horse was sticking into the kitchen from her room.

He was a true gentleman, wearing his three-piece suit with his meticulous vest and gold-chained pocket watch. He agreed to a settlement, and when I asked him for ownership documentation, he advised me there wasn't any papers, but he lived on the land for over thirty years, and before that, his parents occupied the land and used it for growing vegetables for over forty years.

In order to verify the information, I would take the information and have some affidavits prepared and have the owner get two older residents to complete them, attesting to the facts of possession of the property. His parents were deceased, and when I asked him when they died, he told me I would need to see his brother down in the other end of town, as his brother "kept the books" and would know the ages of his parents and the year they passed away. I did this, and sure enough, the brother had a journal that had all the dates I was interested in.

We concluded an agreement with the gentleman the next day, and within the two days, both he and his horse relocated to another location somewhere in the area.

Blowing Up the Doctor's House

I was sent by the government to Marystown to acquire the land for the construction of the Marystown Shipyard. This site was also occupied by a number of homes from which families would have to relocate. Over the years from traveling to the area, I became friends with the medical doctor, and we often had a meal together and a scattered social. He was of Spanish descent and was an excellent cook, and I enjoyed immensely his three-course traditional Spanish dinners (they were more like feasts).

I made very good progress in buying and resettling the families, and the contractor had begun construction on the site but had to work around the few homes for which I was still negotiating. As time went on, I had acquired all the required properties except the home owned by the local doctor (my friend). We just could not reach an amicable agreement. As doctors were hard to get for rural communities, I was aware of this fact and did not want to force the doctor and be responsible if he decided to leave the practice. I returned to St. John's and reported to my boss on the progress and the problem with the one remaining owner, the doctor. My boss went to see the premier, Joey Smallwood to advise him of the situation, and when he returned, he authorized me to return to Marystown and expropriate the doctor's property and give him ten days to vacate.

I made the long, dusty journey back to Marystown and advised my friend that I had no choice but to expropriate his property, as the shipyard development was jeopardized and we had to move on. I advised him of the last date he could remain in possession and urged him to be moved out by that date. I then returned to St. John's, and ten days later, I returned to Marystown to see if the Doctor had moved. I discovered that he had not, and he was gone away somewhere, but nobody knew how to get hold of him. By this time, construction had taken place all around this home, and it was accessible only by a narrow driveway, which the contractor left in the middle of the huge excavation. The contractor's representative advised me that they would have to shut down the project if they didn't have the house removed within another day.

I asked the contractor to provide a truck and a few men and to remove all the contents of the doctor's home to a dry secure storage, which we had arranged. This was done, and all the possessions were carefully removed to the new storage area. When I gave the clearance to the contractor to take over the property and remove the home, he called in his explosive superintendent and told him to destroy the home and remove it from the site. The superintendent loaded up the house with dynamite, boarded up all the windows and any other openings, and fired the explosion. The result was one gigantic bang, and the largest piece of debris to fall back to earth was the size of a split.

Mission accomplished, until an hour later, when I got back to my boarding house to find that lots of property owners in Marystown wanted to see me. I arranged meetings with them and, one by one, was advised that the explosion had broken dishes, cracked walls and ceilings and a few foundations, and god knows what else in an area up to a mile from the explosion. I was six months settling damage claims as a result of this explosion. I noticed soon after that the explosives superintendent for the company was no longer employed on the job!

CHAPTER 7
WORKING IN SOCIAL HOUSING

The Rat

During the early 1970s, I worked at the Newfoundland and Labrador Housing as its real estate manager. There were only a few staff members and many clients. Sometimes the clients became frustrated waiting for their application for housing to be processed or waiting for a repair to an existing Newfoundland and Labrador Housing unit, which they occupied. This caused some of them to come up with unique ways to get the attention they were seeking. There were many amusing incidents from those days. Some were not funny at the time, but in retrospect, you can see the humor in it.

My boss was a rather timid guy, and his office was next to mine. One day I heard loud voices, a bang, and some sort of commotion in his office. I went out to investigate and found that a tenant in one of the corporation's social housing units, who was a former well-known athlete, had not been satisfied with the response he had received over a complaint that there were rodents in his home. He brought a dead rat with him and slammed it on the supervisor's desk to show him the size of the rodents that were in his unit.

Once the startled supervisor, who had already jumped away from his desk, regained his composure, he advised the tenant that he would make sure the problem was looked after that day. This satisfied the client, and he gathered up the rat put it into a bag and left.

The supervisor was still shaken up, and after the client had left, he asked me if I could make sure someone visited that unit immediately and look after the problem that existed there. He certainly didn't want anymore rats put on his desk.

Can't Get My Arm Over My Head

I was sent to an outport community to interview a couple who had applied for a forgivable loan to make renovations to his home. To be eligible for funding under this program, you had to have a handicap that prohibited you from working.

When I arrived at the home in Trinity Bay on a nice sunny summer afternoon, I located the owner of the house out in the yard doing some maintenance. The house was a beautiful well-maintained bungalow, and I could see that the basement was being dug out.

The owner came out to meet me, and I advised him that I was here to interview him for the loan for which he had applied. He started telling me why he could not work and said that he could not raise his arm up over his head. He then commenced to show me all the excavation he had done himself in digging out his basement by hand, and while telling me, he raised his arm up in a gesture to show me the difficulty he had in raising his arm, but he got carried away in his enthusiasm and raised his arm well above his head. Based on his obvious agility and seeing all the digging and shoveling he did and how well he had maintained his house and garden, it was very difficult for him to convince me that he was handicapped to the point where he could qualify for the loan.

When I made my report recommending against the loan and advised the owner that it had not been approved, he advised me that he understood, and we did not hear from him after that.

Gone Moose Hunting

I was sent to Badger to investigate a report from the local council that one of the social housing units in the town was starting to look shabby and dilapidated. The large living room window was broken out, and the curtains were blowing out through the window.

I checked the file and got a picture of the lovely bungalow surrounded by a nice wood picket fence. This would help me find the home when I arrived in the town. When I did get there, I drove up and down the main road several times, but there was no house matching the one in the photo. I went to the town hall and asked for directions, and the clerk stepped outside to point out the house to me. I had already driven past it a few times but did not recognize it. There was no picket fence in evidence; it had been completely removed and used for firewood, and the house was indeed dilapidated looking.

I knocked on the front door, and it was answered by a lady, and when I advised her I was with the Newfoundland and Labrador Housing Corporation, she invited me in. I asked if I could conduct an inspection, which she agreed to, and I did a walkthrough of the interior to assess its condition. I could not believe the mess the house was in. There were two kids wearing knee-high rubber boots jumping on the master bed. There was filth on the floor, and I asked the tenant if the toilet was working, as the house was connected to the municipal water and sewer system. She advised me that it was working okay.

When I went to the living room the whole windowpane was missing, and I asked how long it had been broken and was advised it had been out for several weeks. I inquired why her husband had not boarded it over to keep the weather out, and she said that he did not have any wood. I asked to see him and was told he was gone to the Avalon area moose hunting and would not be home for several days.

My social conscience was stretched to the limit, and I had a difficult time authorizing the window replacement, and except for the welfare of the children and the mother, I probably would not have done so.

"The Mainland Inspector"

While working at the Newfoundland and Labrador Housing Corporation as the real estate manager, I had to deal with CMHC to obtain funding for joint projects between the government of Canada and the province of Newfoundland to build affordable housing units in areas where they were needed.

One February day, I got a phone call from one of the CMHC supervisors, a Mr. Ray Comfrey, from the CMHC head office in Ottawa saying that he wanted to come to Newfoundland to see some of the projects they were funding jointly with us at NLHC. I agreed that this was a good idea but requested that he wait until summertime when travel conditions would be better than they presently were as there was still lots of snow around. He agreed, but within a few weeks, he was pressing me to come here. He wanted to see some of the projects on the Burin Peninsula. I finally agreed, and we arranged a convenient time during the month of April.

Ray had never been to Newfoundland before, and I advised him that the springtime is not the best time to come to visit the Burin Peninsula due to the gravel highway becoming rough and sometimes impassable for periods of time.

He insisted on coming anyway. He arranged his travel and advised me when he would be arriving, and I agreed to pick him up at St. John's Airport and drive him to Burin, Marystown, Fortune, and Grand Bank. When he arrived, I brought him to a local hotel for the night, and the next day, I rented a car and picked him up.

The weather was raining, and traveling on the gravel Burin Peninsula highway was messy. We were getting mud from vehicles passing in the other direction and, from time to time, from vehicles in front of us that I caught up with. We finally arrived in Marystown at the end of the day and stayed there for the first night. The next day, we went on to Grand Bank and Fortune. We toured the projects, and he was more than pleased with the quality of the workmanship of the housing units and with the management of them.

The weather was cold, and it had been raining for the two days we were there. Sometime during the second day, I dropped into the local highways depot and was advised by an official that the Burin Peninsula Highway had become washed out in a few places, and it was becoming difficult for vehicles to get through. In another day, it would likely have to be closed. I advised Ray, and he stated that he was on a tight schedule and couldn't afford to be stuck on the peninsula for a few days, so we decided we had better leave to get back while the road was passable.

We drove for an hour or so, and when we arrived in Bay L'Argent, we found that the road had been turned into a complete mud quagmire and a number of cars and trucks were stuck in it. We had a look at the situation and helped drag and push a few vehicles for a while, but it was impossible to move these by hand as they were stuck so deeply.

I sized up the situation and decided that I didn't have anything to lose by trying my luck to get through the area. I advised Ray to hold on and I would get a run and see if I could make it through. I skidded back and forth but somehow managed to keep moving and cavorted around cars and trucks often with only inches to spare and luckily made it safely to the other side.

We stopped to see if we could help anyone else, and another car decided that as I made it safely through, he would give it a try. He headed into the mud hole, which it had become by now, and after a few feet, he became solidly stuck in mud up to his bumper. He was in the last remaining area where a car could possibly get through, so he effectively had finally fully closed the highway.

There being nothing further we could do to assist anybody, we decided to carry on and made our way to Swift Current, the next place where we could stop and get gas and a snack. As there was a clunking sound coming from the engine compartment while driving, when I stopped, I decided to lift the bonnet and check to see if everything was OK. When I did, to my surprise, I found the battery hanging suspended only by the battery cables. I put it back into its cradle and secured it and was very thankful that it had held on through all the rough road we had driven over.

I could tell that Ray was nervous because, during the entire ride, he had his hands firmly clutched onto the car dash. Needless to say, he was completely relieved when I told him that we had arrived back to the paved Trans-Canada Highway. I am sure that the prints of his hands were forever imbedded on that car's dash.

I took him safely home to St. John's and brought him to his hotel for the night. He flew back to Ottawa the next day. I am sure he had an unbelievable story to tell his colleagues about his experience traveling in Newfoundland. During my four years as the real estate manager, I did not have any further requests from officials in Ottawa to come to see any of our projects in Newfoundland and Labrador. I wonder why!

Living in the Basement Foundation

One fine summer day, I was dispatched to Catalina to interview a couple for a loan. As I drove up and down the street where they said they lived, I could not find any homes on it. After a few more drives, I observed a concrete basement that looked like it was boarded over, and I noticed someone out in the backyard area. I went in and asked if the lady knew where the home was that I was looking for, and she advised me that this was it. She called to her husband, who came out to greet me.

They advised me that they saved enough money to have a foundation poured, and as they had nowhere to live, they had it boarded over and were living in it. After interviewing them and being satisfied that they were genuine, and they qualified for the loan, I gladly approved them a mortgage to finish their home. When I went back next year to conduct an inspection, I was pleased that they had built a lovely modest home on the site.

Photographed by Bill Peckham while he was in the Air Force

Cadet of the Year 1956-57
P.O. Don Peckham & Cdr. George G.R. Parsons

1986 Don Peckham
Trout caught in Churchill Falls, Labrador

The Cabot Club (Hotel Newfoundland) 1988
Front Right - Don Peckham

Leading Cadet Don Peckham
Enroute HMCS Acadia   1955

On right -Commander Don Peckham
General Support Force Atlantic Exercise - 1988

NEWFOUNDLAND AND LABRADOR COMPUTER SERVICES LIMITED
BOARD OF DIRECTORS

Back row, left to right:
• D.R. Keats • D. Peckham • W. Thistle • E. Drodan

Front row, left to right:
• D.W. Osmond • E. Marshall • H. Miller • D. Roberts • R.O. Pettigrew • M.M. O'Dea • R. Grouchy

Don Peckham
Naval base - Bristol, England 1997

L-R: Debbie Hanlon; James Cameron, Movie producer/Director; Don Peckham
Aboard the Russian Research Ship Akademik Kaeldic

Don Peckham 2008

International Chartered Secretaries and Administrators Executive

Front L-R: ? Collins; Don Peckham; Dan Wong
Rear L - R ? ; ? ; Frank Wright; ? ; Frank Burridge
Abt. 1995

Don Peckham - Florida 1999

CHAPTER 8
GENERAL INTEREST

Exploits Boat Ride

One of my friends, Dave Gilbert, who was living in central Newfoundland, was the owner of a very nice yacht. One summer, he invited me and another friend, Reuben Harding, to come for a weekend cruising up the Exploits River to the abandoned community of Exploits. I was delighted to take him up on his offer, and at the end of a working week, my friend and I drove from St. John's to Botwood to meet with Dave and proceed on the cruise. We arrived in Botwood that afternoon, loaded our supplies on board, did the necessary checks of the engine and other areas of the boat, and left for Exploits. The trip up the river was beautiful. The lush green trees lining the banks of the river with a few houses here and there was a very pleasant sight.

Somewhere along the way, the boat engine began to act up, and Maurice and myself lifted the hatch and started to examine the engine to see if we could find out what the problem was. We had to climb down into the cramped engine compartment to examine the engine, the fuel pump, water pump, spark plugs, etc.

The fumes were heavy, and we were glad when we could get up out of the compartment. We didn't find anything serious, so we packed up the tools we were using and proceeded back on deck. After a few minutes, Dave said that he wasn't feeling well and was going below to lie down for a while. After a few more minutes, I also became ill and was losing my balance and could not see clearly. I decided to go below to check on my friend, only to find him in a bad way, shaking uncontrollably and feeling very ill.

When we reached the abandoned community of Exploits, Reuben, who was driving the boat, called me to ask where we were going to tie up in Exploits. As neither he nor I had been there before, we were not familiar with the docking options. I looked around and suggested that we go to a nearby vacant wharf and hope there would be someone in the area that could offer us some help. He needed me to assist with getting the boat into the wharf. I could barely focus but managed to call out some directions as we neared the wharf and docked there. I somehow got on the wharf and tied our boat on.

There was nobody around to help us. So Reuben and I had a discussion as to what was the best course of action for us to take. It was late afternoon, and we could not make it back to Botwood before dark. Neither of us knew the area, and we were concerned about trying to find our way back in the dark. However, I was not very well, and Dave was even in worse condition. We decided we had no reasonable option but to head back and hope we could find the way and not run aground in the darkness. Dave was too ill to come on deck to help, but we decided to push on.

We headed off with my friend driving the boat and me on the bow deck watching where we were going and taking bearings as best I could from headland to headland and directing the driver where to go. This was very tiring for me, as I had difficulty focusing, and it was a great strain trying to see the points of land and the scattered shore lights.

After several gruelling hours and with a great deal of luck, we arrived back in Botwood harbour about ten o'clock that evening. It was pitch-black, and we did not know where the government wharf was located. We continued to cruise along until finally I spotted the government wharf and directed my friend to steer to it.

When we arrived, I climbed onto the wharf with a rope to secure our boat. I managed to put it around a bollard and then I passed out on the wharf. After a while, I came to and could stand up and was feeling a bit better.

We got Dave into a taxi and had him delivered to the Botwood Hospital where he was detained overnight. By the next day, we had both recovered. The medical people at the hospital were convinced that we either had suffered from food poisoning or carbon monoxide poisoning. They took samples of all the food we had on board plus our drinks and had them shipped to a Halifax laboratory for testing. When the results were received several weeks later, they advised there was no problem with any of the food or beverage.

Having this report, the medical staff could only conclude that we both suffered from carbon monoxide poisoning. This probably happened as the two of us were working down in the hole with the engine running. It was located near the stern of the boat, and exhaust from the engine could easily have been drawn into the engine compartment while we were working there.

Reuben and I never did get to enjoy the lovely Exploits community, but I was very happy that both Dave and I made a full recovery. I counted myself as lucky to have survived the ordeal, which could easily have ended more disastrously for us.

Gilbert Hay's Art Sculpture

While I was chairman of the government's Art Procurement Committee, we decided to commission the creation of a few major sculpture works, which would be lasting tributes to the artists, and a showcase for unique Newfoundland and Labrador artists' works.

One of these commissions was awarded to artist Gilbert Hay in Nain, Labrador. It was to be a granite sculpture of a whale and some other marine life. Gilbert agreed to the commission, which was to be carved from a solid piece of stone weighing about two tons.

I had arranged to have the rock quarried from an area in Baie Verte, which had good stone for this purpose and then to have it transported from Baie Verte to Nain. Gilbert said that he could create the sculpture in one year. I followed up by telephone with Gilbert to track the progress of the sculpture, and we would give him money advances as the work progressed.

After seven or eight months Gilbert was getting very difficult to reach by telephone, and I soon became worried that something had gone wrong with the sculpture or perhaps Gilbert had given up on it.

When the summer arrived, I had an opportunity to visit Nain on other government business but was glad, as I would have a chance to visit Gilbert and see how the sculpture was coming along. I flew from St. John's to Happy Valley-Goose Bay and then by a smaller airplane from Goose Bay to various Labrador coastal communities, and we would eventually end up in Nain.

In the meantime, we had intended to stop for the night at a camp in Voisey's Bay. The weather was good, and the Labrador scenery flying over it was just spectacular. When we arrived in the area of Voisey's Bay, we had to find the location of the camp. As none of us had been there before, we decided to fly low up and down the river to see if we could spot the camp.

After several flyovers, we did not see the camp and were starting to get worried that we would not find it and have to go on to Nain for the night. We decided to have one more fly around when one of the passengers spotted a building near the bank of the river. After flying over it, we were satisfied that it looked like the facility and location that was described to us, and we decided to land the float plane in the river and taxi into the wharf near the camp.

When we got out of the plane and walked the few hundred feet to the camp, we were indeed very happy. The camp was a modern building and, inside it, had a large stone wall-to-wall fireplace. It had a full kitchen and several bedrooms.

We unloaded our personal effects from the airplane and settled in the camp for the evening and a planned barbecue. While doing this, the pilot approached me and advised that he needed to go to Nain to fuel the airplane as his company had fuel stored there. He said that he was extremely low on fuel and wanted to go to Nain with a light load and while the weather was favorable.

He asked if I wanted to come along, but I had enough flying for the day and decided to stay at the camp with the rest of our crew. The pilot said that he would go on as he had a fellow in Nain that would help him with the fueling, and he would be back in an hour or so before the evening closed in and it got dark.

The pilot left around six o'clock, and we started to prepare for our barbecue supper. We had some steaks and a few baked potatoes, and they were delicious. After an hour and a half passed, I became worried about the pilot, as he had not yet returned, and he had advised that he would not stay at Nain and would return as soon as possible. Another half hour passed, and there was no sign of the airplane returning.

I did not want to cause any worry with the rest of my crew but had spoken to one or two of them and expressed a cautious concern. In another fifteen minutes, I heard the sound of an airplane engine and immediately went outside and was quite relieved when I saw our airplane approaching and landing in the lake.

When the pilot came in, I told him that I was becoming concerned about his safety, and he told me the story of what he had to do. He arrived in Nain but could not find the person that was responsible for assisting with the fuelling. He ended up getting someone to take him from his airplane pontoon and bring him ashore and get a forty-five-gallon drum of fuel and bring it out to the airplane. He then had to pump the fuel by hand with a small pump he had on board. This took a considerable time, and it had to be repeated a couple of times to fill the fuel tanks.

This took him a lot longer than it normally would, and it delayed his return, and he was concerned he would not make it back before dark and he would have had to wait overnight in Nain, as he could not fly the airplane in the dark.

The next morning, we left Voisey's Bay camp and headed for Nain. We landed the plane in Nain harbor, got one of the local residents to come out and take us ashore, and we then proceeded to Gilbert's home to view the work. When I arrived there, I was advised that Gilbert wasn't home and that he wasn't expected back for a few days or so. Apparently, he had left to go hunting, and his wife did not know just when he would arrive back home. She said that when he went, sometimes it was a week before he returned home.

I asked her if I could see the work, and she said, "No problem, come on into the house and have a look at it." Inside the bungalow, Gilbert had this huge stone piece in the living room with a partly carved whale.

The stone was much too large to have been brought in through the door, so I asked Mrs. Hay how Gilbert got it in there. She said that he had sawed out the wall in the living room and had the stone brought in and then put back the wall of the house. When the work was finished, he intended to again cut out the wall to get it out.

In any event, the work took a bit longer than planned to be completed, but it eventually was, and I arranged to have it shipped from Nain to the Confederation Building, West Block, where it was installed in the main lobby. It is still there today.

It is a beautiful work of art and is a credit to the work and skill of Mr. Gilbert Hay.

A Unique Land Survey

I came across this "certified land survey" in some file I was handling. It would have been accurate at the time the ranger did it, but I would imagine that it would be difficult to follow the description now. It also shows the diversity of activities the Newfoundland Rangers would have to perform in their line of duty back in 1945. It is certainly a unique survey containing some unique terminology.

Land at Red Bay—

Land, beginning at a point on the northerly side of the road which runs from the United Church in the general direction of the home of John Pike. Said point, hereinafter called Point 1, can be fixed by triangulation. It is 88 feet in a general NW direction from a large rock about the size of four puncheons, and 66 feet in a general N direction from the most westerly of four rocks (Those 4 rocks are close together and in line, the rocks at either end are larger than barrels and the two in the middle are smaller.

From Point 1 the land runs 150 feet in a general NW direction to point 2. Point 2 is 46 feet from the present location of the church flagpole, and 34 feet from the northerly corner of the Ranger Force Storehouse.

From point 2 the land takes a port turn and follows the brow of the hill, until said brow meets the aforementioned road which runs from the church in the general direction of John Pike's. It meets said road at point 7.

Point 7 is 103 feet from point 1.

From point 2 to point 7, following the brow of the hill, the land passes through points 3, 4, 5 and 6. These points have been designated by wooden markers driven into the ground. From point 5 to point 6, the land passes close behind, and immediately above the house of John Pike.

Point 3 is approx. 90 feet from point 2.

Point 4 is approx. 46 feet from Point 3.

Point 5 is approx. 46 feet from point 4.

Point 5 Plus 1 (that is point 6) is approx. 40 feet from point 5.

Point 7 is approx. 66 feet from point 6.

Certified correct

Signed by E. Delaney, Sergt. Reg #16, Newfoundland Ranger Force. 31-10-45.

I have left the abbreviations and all wording exactly as he had written them.

The Tip

Many times I would travel with government ministers, and we would inevitably end up entertaining a group that we were meeting with. The ministers had an entertainment allowance that they could use for this purpose, and as an executive member of government, I could also pay for a meal for people that we were meeting within the course of our business.

Normally when the minister was present, he would pick up the bill and get reimbursed for it later. However, Honorable Ed Maynard used to like to play jokes on me, and sometimes I would repay him with a joke of my own. It was all in fun. Eventually, it became a game to see who could get who first.

This minister was a clever guy, and one day, we were at a hotel where we needed to buy dinner for our meeting group. We were just about finished dinner when he looked at me and said, "Don, I will pay the bill and you pick up the tip."

When the bill arrived, he paid the amount of the meal, and when I asked the waiter the total amount so I could leave a tip, she told me the tip on meals for about fifteen people was considerable. Of course, I paid it and immediately realized the minister had tricked me as he knew that he could claim the cost of the meal but I was not entitled to claim a tip for a meal for which I did not pay.

I enjoyed the meal, but needless to say, the tip cost a lot more than if I had to purchase my own meal. I was always careful with him after that when I went out to dinner with him and a group.

Lady Stuck in a Sewer Pipe

I owned a mobile home in Florida for a number of years, and occasionally friends and relatives would come to stay with us for a vacation.

On one such occasion, a good friend of mine, Reuben, and his lovely wife, Mable, were visiting; and I took advantage of their time with me to do some much-needed repairs to the unit.

We decided to upgrade the bathroom and had to take out the toilet and replace it with a new, more efficient one. The temperature was about thirty degrees centigrade, or ninety-two degrees Fahrenheit. We had to work outside under the unit to remove some old sewer piping and replace it. In order to do so, it was necessary to crawl under the unit, which was about one foot off the ground on the gravel.

I wondered about the possibility of there being snakes in there, as they were not uncommon in the area, and there were many other types of spiders and insects that we were not used to. But necessity required me to get in there and cut the old pipes and rejoin the new ones.

In the meantime, before starting this job, someone noticed that the telephone was not working, so I had to use a neighbor's phone and call Verizon to come and check on the problem with the phone. Reuben and I had the toilet removed and had crawled under the unit to replace the sewer pipe. When this was done, we went into the bathroom to put the toilet back on. I noticed that the new pipe had a ragged edge and asked Reuben to pass me a large steel file so I could file the pipe smooth before installing the toilet.

He passed me a file, and I began to file, but with the heat, my hands were wet and the file slipped out of my hand and went down the drainpipe. I tried to reach it, but my hand was too large to go around the ninety-degree angle in the pipe. Reuben tried, and he also could not get his hand down far enough to get the file out.

Reuben said that his wife had smaller hands and arms, and he would get her to try to reach it for us. Well, she got her arm into the pipe and around the ninety-degree angle and said she could feel the file, but then discovered she could not get her hand back out of the pipe. We were in a bit of a spot trying everything possible to help her get her hand out of the pipe, but we were not successful.

So there she was on her hands and knees, arse up in the air, with her arm caught down the sewer pipe. We decided we would have to go back under the unit and carefully saw off the pipe. So out we went and squeezed back under the unit, sweat rolling off both of us and dirt from the sandy clay sticking all over us.

Then I heard a vehicle pull up and someone called out looking for Mr. Peckham. I crawled out from under the unit, and the person told me he was from the phone company and wanted to go inside to check on the telephone problem. In order to do so, he would have to pass the bathroom, and surely, he would wonder what the lady was doing on her hands and knees with her bum sticking up in the air. I wondered how to handle this situation, so I hurriedly went in and told Mable that I would have to close the bathroom door for a short time while the telephone men were working on the phone problem.

It didn't take long when the phone guy came over and advised me that he had the problem fixed. When I asked him what the problem was, he advised that someone had replaced the phone in the kitchen upside down on the receiver, and the system had cut the line so as not to have it left in an open position.

Needless to say, this was embarrassing. I was conscious of Mable still stuck in the sewer pipe. The phone company technician noted that we had an accent different from his and asked where we were from. I really did not want to tell him, fearing it could become another Newfoundland joke, so I told him we were from Canada. He was not satisfied with such a general answer as Canada and asked from what part. I decided to tell him we were from Ontario in the event he knew about Newfoundland and could add it as another Newfie joke.

He finally departed, and we commenced to try to get Mable's arm loose. We made a bucket of soapy water and poured it down the drain over her arm and asked her to turn it around a few times, and much to our relief, she managed to pull it clear. But she did not have the file in her hand.

We decided there would be no more arms going down to look for the file, so we went back under the unit in the sweltering heat and cut off the brand-new pipe and retrieved the file. We put a new joiner on the pipe and came back in to finish the toilet installation. Needless to say, I held tightly on to the file to complete the job, and eventually, we finished the job.

After a good cold shower and a cool beverage, we sat with the ladies and laughed our heads off over the circumstances of the day.

My Father's Ingenuity

My father was, as they say, a jack of all trades, which was a necessity for many fathers raising a family from the 1930s to the 1960s. While he worked at a full-time day job, he had a number of extracurricular activities that enabled him to supplement his income. He built chimneys for new homes, and he manufactured terrazzo fireplaces, which were installed in new homes. Sometimes he found it difficult to collect payment for his work after the job was completed, and he became creative in his methods to ensure payment. In one instance, he was asked to build a chimney for a lady who had a reputation for not paying for work done for her. My father could not let the opportunity to make an extra dollar go by, so he took the job for a fixed price. When the job was completed, the lady did not have the payment available and told father she would pay him at a later date. Two days later, Father got a panic call from the lady saying that the chimney would not work as when she lit the fireplace, the living room filled up with smoke. Father told her he would come over and discuss the problem with her. He told her that when she paid for the work, he would guarantee that he would get the fireplace working properly. She paid him the money, and Father went out into the garden, picked up a large rock, went upon the roof, and dropped the rock down the chimney. A large crash was heard, and Father told her to light the fireplace and try it out. It worked perfectly. Father had placed a pane of glass across the chimney halfway up when he built it, and when he broke the pane, the chimney was in fine working order.

I Held Up an Airplane

Late in the winter, I had to go to Ottawa for a meeting with Parks Canada. It was near spring, and the weather was changing. While in Ottawa, the temperature was quite mild, and when I was at the airport to leave for home, I decided to put my parka, which I had on, into my suitcase.

The airplane was on time, and we soon departed for Newfoundland. It was an uneventful flight, but as we approached Deer Lake, I could see that the weather there was nasty. It was ten thirty in the night, freezing cold, with blistering snow.

When I disembarked the airplane in my shirtsleeves, I regretted that I had put my parka into the suitcase, as I now had to stand outside in the snowstorm, waiting for my baggage to get at my parka. In those days, the luggage ramp at Deer Lake Airport was outside the building. Only a handful of passengers got off the plane, which was carrying on to St. John's. I waited, shivering, for my bag to be unloaded, but when all the bags were placed on the ramp, mine was not there.

To complicate matters further, my car was parked on the airport parking lot, but my keys were in my parka pocket in my suitcase. The airplane, a 737 Eastern Provincial Airlines flight, closed the door and began to increase the engine speed. I thought for a second that I was going to be left stranded late in the night without any over clothes on the parking lot of the airport.

My instinct kicked in. In those days, there was very little security at Deer Lake Airport, so I dashed in through the building and out the back door and ran out in front of the plane, waving to the pilot. He must have thought I was some kind of a mad man out on the airport in front of a 737 jet on a cold wintery night in my shirt sleeves waving down the airplane.

Luckily, the pilot opened the door, and a crew member came out to see what the problem was. I told him my predicament and stressed that I had to get my suitcase from the airplane before it left for St. John's. Much to my surprise, he called the ground crew, and they opened the cargo door and, in a few minutes, came out carrying my suitcase.

Needless to say, I was more than relieved and very much appreciative of the cooperation of the pilot and crew of Eastern Provincial Airways that night. Can you imagine ever trying that with today's security measures? I probably would have been arrested and spent the night in Deer Lake lockup instead of being able to drive home to Rocky Harbour.

My Frustrating Boat Purchase

When I moved to Gros Morne National Park to work and live, it provided an opportune time for me to buy a boat to be able to explore and enjoy the magnificent bays from Norris Point to Woody Point in the Northeast Arm of Bonne Bay. I could launch in Norris Point and travel anywhere in the bay, do a little mackerel fishing or jig a codfish, and go to some remote cove and have a picnic.

I happened to be in Halifax and got invited to a friend's home for dinner. When I arrived there, I was impresses by the canoes, kayaks, and a speedboat all in his driveway. During dinner, I inquired about his boating, and he advised me he didn't use the spiffy red-and-white speedboat as he and his wife loved to canoe and kayak in the lakes around Nova Scotia. I half jokingly asked if he would consider selling the speedboat to me. I really liked the look of it with its impressive large engine and canopy top.

After some discussion, he said, "Yes, I would sell it," and before the evening was over, we had made a deal, and I became the owner of my first power boat. The next morning, I went to a local garage and had them put a trailer hitch on my car and then went and took delivery of the boat. I was on vacation on my way to Bar Harbour, Maine, so off I went with boat on trailer in tow.

After a few days, when it was time to return to Canada, I noticed the licence plate for the trailer was missing. I wondered how I was going to explain to the US Customs people that I owned the boat and did not purchase it in the United States. I had not gotten a receipt from my friend when I purchased the boat and had nothing to show that I had bought it in Canada. Well, I arrived at the US/ Canadian border at Calais, Maine, and presented my passport and answered a few questions, and the agent said, "You are all clear to go." That was a big relief as he had not questioned me about the boat ownership.

A few days later, on my way to get the ferry from North Sydney to Port Aux Basque, I had some spare time, and while driving along the side of the Bras d'Or Lake, I thought it would be a good time to launch my boat and try it out. I found an area where I could back into the lake and launch the boat off the trailer. So I slowly backed my Oldsmobile into the lake until I was far enough for the boat to float off the trailer. I got out and untied the boat from the trailer and pushed it off and hauled it onto the shore. I then had to drive the car to a safe parking spot, but when I tried to drive it forward, it merely skidded and sunk into the rocks on the bottom of the lake. The more I tried to drive out, the more the car became stuck. Finally, I had to give up and get into the boat and drive to a nearby community and arrange for a tow truck to go and pull my car out of the lake. That was a bit of an embarrassment situation, but I soon got over it as I enjoyed speeding around the lake in my new toy.

I was beginning to wonder if anything was ever going to work well for me with the boat. Anyway, the boat worked swell, and with its powerful engine, I enjoyed a few rides around the lake. When I was finished, I was careful not to back the car too far into the lake to get the boat back on to the trailer, and that went well. I just pulled unto the highway when I heard a siren, and as I looked in my rearview mirror, I saw a police car immediately behind me. I could not think of anything I had done wrong and wondered why he was pulling me in. I moved safely off the highway, and the RCMP constable came over and asked me for my driver's licence and insurance. I was not concerned as I had both. He then informed me that he noticed I did not have a licence plate on the trailer. I explained to him that it was indeed licenced, but somewhere along the way, the plate came off and was lost, and I intended to have it replaced as soon as I arrived home in Rocky Harbour. He advised me that I could not continue with the trailer, as it did not have a licence plate on it.

I did not know what to do, as I was scheduled to catch the ferry that night. I explained this to the officer, but he was adamant that I could not proceed on with the unlicensed trailer. I started to unhook it while I was thinking about how best I could proceed. In the meantime, the police car drove away and left me there alone with my problem. As soon as he got out of sight, I figured the only sensible thing I could do was hitch the trailer back on and carry on the North Sydney. This is what I did, and luckily, I did not encounter that policeman nor any other, and I arrived safely at the ferry terminal. A day later, I was safely home in Rocky Harbour. I was beginning to wonder if this boat thing was going to work out or if it would continue to be a source of problems and frustrations. Fortunately, it worked out well, and I had many years of pleasure cruising around Bonne Bay, watching schools of mackerel, the odd whale, and just enjoying the magnificent scenery in the area.

CHAPTER 9
"SAFE" CIVIL SERVICE JOB

Working in the Public Service

I worked in the public service for thirty-eight years in what most people would have thought was a safe job. Such was not always the case. One of my jobs was as the director of expropriations for the province. This meant that whenever a government department needed a parcel of land for any purpose, i.e., for road construction or widening, housing development, hospital construction, building a government building such as Confederation Building, or for some other economic development activity; and the officials could not purchase it by direct negotiations, mostly for a paltry sum they would offer the owner, the government would legally take it by expropriating it.

Once expropriated, title legally transferred to the government, and it could go ahead and use it for the purpose for which it needed it. In the meantime, I would have to try to negotiate an agreement with the owner as to the amount of compensation they would receive for it. This was not always easy, as by now, the owner was angry with the government for taking their property rather than negotiating a purchase beforehand.

Don't Come Any Further or I'll Shoot

One of the projects I was asked to expropriate the property for was to acquire a right of way easement to install a water and sewer line in Catalina. I negotiated as many of the easements as possible, and most of the owners were more than cooperative, as they were going to get the benefit of having a water and sewer system service for their house for the first time.

However, there were always a few owners that did not want to give the right of way through their property for various reasons. After I had exhausted all attempts at negotiating, we had to resort to expropriating the land. In such cases, the title was legally taken from the owner, but they were still compensated fair market value for it.

In one such case in Catalina, I had to resort to expropriating a right of way through the back garden of the owner who was not happy with this. However, the land was acquired, and I advised the Department of Municipal Affairs that they could award the contract for the system as all the needed right of way had been secured.

This was done, and a contract awarded for the work. About two weeks later, I received a phone call at my office. It was the contractor that was installing the water and sewer line. The contractor advised me that his tractor operator was proceeding along the right of way installing the pipes, and they came to the property of one of the owners who was standing by his fence with a rifle aimed at the tractor operator. He advised the operator not to proceed through his yard or he would stop him. The tractor operator telephoned his boss to ask what he should do. The company owner advised me of the situation and asked what the operator should do. I advised him that it seemed prudent to me that he stop his tractor from going through that yard and call the police to the scene.

The RCMP eventually arrived, and when they could not convince the owner to put down his gun, they called in some reinforcements and were able to talk the gentleman into putting down his gun, and they arrested him and took him to the local lockup for questioning. I was informed that the gentleman had been taken in by the police and that they would hold him overnight.

I immediately called the contractor and advised him of this and suggested he go through that property and install the lines and restore the property to its original condition. They did this and replaced his fence and sods. The next day, the gentleman was released, and when advised that the pipes were laid and his garden restored, he couldn't believe it. When he had a look at it, he said that they did a good job, and he was no longer concerned.

Shortly after that, I visited him and was able to reach an amicable agreement on compensation for the right of way.

Sometimes ingenious ways had to be made to obtain the desired results and, in the end, all would turn out well.

I Will Shoot You

On another occasion, I was acquiring property to develop the Beothic Provincial Park on Rushy Pond near Grand Falls. There were several cottages in the area that had to be acquired and removed to make way for the development. Again, most of the owners were cooperative, but in this case, one of them resisted the acquisition.

The owner was a very prominent businessperson, and each time I spoke with him, he became agitated and would not negotiate and advised he would never let his property go. After several attempts to meet with him to negotiate and each time he would tell me he had no intention of meeting, I advised him we would have to expropriate the property.

I had the expropriation notices prepared and arranged to have them served on the gentleman. Afterward, I called him to explain the process for compensating him and asked if I could come to see him to start the process. He advised me in an angry tone that if I came to see him that he would shoot me.

I was not sure if he was serious or just being brave, but I did not have any intention of finding out. Whenever I needed to contact him in the future, I did it by telephone and/or in writing. Mostly it was in writing, as he was never calm enough and was always threatening when I spoke with him on the phone.

Eventually, he engaged a lawyer to represent him, and after that, we were able to arrive at an agreement as to the amount of compensation to pay him for the property.

To this day, I was never sure if his threat to use the gun was serious or not, but with the tones of his speech when we talked, there seemed a reasonable possibility that he was capable of doing it, and I was glad that I never had to find out.

Lady with the Butchers Knife

On another occasion, I visited a lady in her home in Stephenville and advised her I was there to expropriate some of the frontage of her land to allow for the road to be widened in the area. As soon as she heard this, she grabbed a butcher knife from her kitchen counter and chased me out of her home. It didn't take me long to exit the home, as I was unarmed and had nothing with which I could defend myself.

After a week or so, I contacted her by phone, and by then, she was more reasonable and we were able to agree on the amount of compensation she would be paid for the loss of the land and injurious affection due to the new road being built so close to her home.

The $700,000 Duck

Gerry Conran and I were traveling together on business and boarded a flight from Stephenville to St. John's after a week traveling the West Coast and the Northern Peninsula. As it was the end of the week, we were glad to be finally on the way home. It was a beautiful sunny day as we waited for the Eastern Provincial Airlines 737 Boeing airplane to arrive.

The plane arrived, and the passengers disembarked, and after a while, we were called to board. The plane taxied down the runway for takeoff. We lifted under full power from the runway and began to climb when suddenly there was an abrupt shudder in the plane, and it tipped to one side and dropped before leveling off again. There was a smell of smoke, and passengers were looking out the windows and someone said that there was a fire.

I looked out the window, and seeing how high we were, I immediately said to Gerry that it is too late; we are too high, and if we crash, we will not survive. A million things flashed through my mind before I realized the plane had leveled off and was still flying.

We turned out over Bay St. George, and the pilot began to discharge some of his fuel to prepare for an emergency landing.

After flying around for twenty or thirty minutes, we were advised to prepare for an emergency landing back at Stephenville Airport. When we approached the airport, I could see the fire trucks lined along the runway awaiting our arrival. The plane touched down without incident and taxied near the terminal building where we disembarked.

Afterwards, inside the airport, I was speaking with a gentleman who advised me that he was flying a small plane at the time of our incident, and our pilot asked him to fly alongside and advise him on the extent of the fire and damage to the airplane. He told me that a section of the engine cowling had been completely ripped from the airplane, and one engine had been dislodged from its main bearings.

I went out to see the damage afterward and could not believe that such a large piece had been torn off the airplane and we were able to fly around and make a safe landing. The small plane pilot told me that a lot of credit was due the pilot of our airplane, as he managed to keep her in the air after such an incident while still under full takeoff power.

Sometime after the incident, I met Harry Steele, Eastern Provincial Airlines owner, and I told him that I had been on the plane that had the incident while taking off in Stephenville a few weeks before. He told me that the plane had taken a duck into the engine and that duck cost him seven hundred thousand dollars in repairs.

The Grievance

I received a phone call from the principal of the Vocational Training School in St. Anthony advising me that somebody was stealing liquor from a locked cabinet in the staff room of the school. The cabinet did not seem to be broken into, and the lock was still on it. He had the lock changed in case someone had obtained a spare key, but the liquor was still going missing every now and then.

He said that he could arrange to have some dye from the RCMP put on the bottles to try to catch the thief. The dye would be invisible to the naked eye but would show up clearly when put under an ultraviolet light. I did not have any problem with this and agreed that he could proceed with the plan.

The principal then marked the level in each bottle and arranged to have the dye put on the bottles. One Monday morning, when he checked the cabinet, he noticed that the liquor had been reduced in the bottles. He arranged to have the ultraviolet light set up in his staff room and had all his staff come through the process to have their hands checked for dye residue. They all went through, but no one had any of the dye on them. The only persons left that could have accessed the property over the weekend were the employees of my department, who were the watchman and maintenance person.

The principal telephoned me to advise of the situation and to request approval to ask my department's staff to go through the screening process. I agreed that I didn't have a problem with this as long as the employees did it voluntarily. After an hour or so, I received another phone call from the principal advising that one of our security personnel had shown the dye on his hands. After questioning, he admitted that he had accessed the cabinet and stole the liquor while he was on the midnight shift from time to time.

He was able to move the cabinet out from the wall and unscrew boards from the back of the cabinet and access the liquor. He helped himself and replaced the boards and moved the cabinet back into its place.

I had the principal confirm the facts for me in writing. When this was received, I had the security person dismissed from his job for breach of trust and theft.

After a while, the employee filed a grievance against his dismissal. A grievance committee was formed, and I was appointed as its chairman with a colleague of mine and a representative of the Newfoundland Association of Public Employees, the union representing the dismissed employee, as the other two members.

Eventually, I had some business to do in Corner Brook and the Deer Lake area, and I decided to tie grievance hearing into that trip. I flew to Deer Lake and spent a day in the Corner Brook area doing staff meetings, and when these were finished, I headed up the Northern Peninsula. I always called it "up the Northern Peninsula" when going north even though I was aware that the locals on the Northern Peninsula always referred to it as "going down the Northern Peninsula" when going north. We arrived at St. Anthony around midday Thursday and had the hearing set for the afternoon.

When the hearing commenced, I asked the griever (the dismissed employee) to state the basis for his appeal. He told us that he did not feel he did anything wrong as the liquor was illegally in the school. I asked him to elaborate, and he said that it is against government policy for anyone to have liquor in a government building. Therefore, he only took something that was not allowed in the building.

It did not seem to occur to him that when he stole the liquor, it was still illegally in a government building, if that were in fact the case. I asked him if he could show me where the government policy was written stating that it was illegal to have liquor in a government building. He said that he did not know where it was written but that everybody knew that this was the government policy.

I advised him that as the assistant deputy minister of the Department of Public Works and Services, I was given the responsibility to develop the policies for operating government buildings and that I had never written such a policy and I was sure that it, in fact, did not exist.

In this case, the staff would have a limited amount of liquor left over from some celebration such as a Christmas party, and they would keep it in a secure, locked cabinet to be used when they had an activity, such as saying farewell to a staff person who was leaving to go to some other posting. There was no problem with this, and it was accepted as normal in such circumstances.

The panel upheld the decision of the department to terminate the employment of the security officer. As we were finished our work for the day, we retired to our hotel for the night and intended to get an early morning start for the long drive back to Deer Lake in the morning. But that provided its own challenges, as you will see in the next story.

Lost on the Great Northern Peninsula

The same colleague that was with me when we had the duck incident in the airplane in Stephenville, Gerry Conran, had been with me in St. Anthony where we were hearing several employee grievances with the Newfoundland Association of Public Employees union. We had finished all the hearings Thursday night and were anxious to get back home in St. John's after being away all week. It was mid-February, and the weather was for a snowstorm to move in during the morning. We decided to get up early and leave before the storm made the road too treacherous to drive. I looked out the hotel window, and a blowing snowstorm had already started. Against our better judgment, we left the hotel. We noticed that a considerable amount of snow had already accumulated, and we were not sure if we could race the storm on its southerly path down the Northern Peninsula. I drove to the outskirts of town to the provincial highways depot and went in to check with them to see if they could tell me if the road was suitable for us to travel on. The official advised that he still had his equipment (snow ploughs) on the highway, so we could go on and he would advise his operators we were on the road and to keep an eye out for us.

We left town with an uneasy feeling and, after a short time, felt that we had not made a good decision as we did not encounter any other traffic on the road and the storm had picked up to the extent that we could scarcely see where the road was. We continued along the Northern Peninsula highway, and the snow continued to mount up on the road, and the winds were gusting, creating blinding snow squalls. After twenty minutes or so, we could no longer see the road, then suddenly there was a poof, and we landed down over a ten- to fifteen-foot bank buried in several feet of fresh snow.

There was nothing we could do except put our faith in the fact that the highways operators were aware we were somewhere on the road and would keep a grader on the road until we were found. Luckily, we had a tank full of gasoline and could keep the engine running, with the window ajar so as not to get poisoned by carbon monoxide, and keep us warm. We continued to listen, hoping to hear the snowplough in time for us to get out of the car and up to the road so the operator would see us and stop. Hour after hour passed by, and we realized that there probably were not any snowploughs left on the highway.

After a while, we heard the sound of a vehicle and scrambled up to the road just in time to stop a large transport truck that had braved the weather. It was a wholesale grocery truck, and the driver invited us to go along with him. He was from Flowers Cove and knew the road and felt that he could make it through with his heavy truck. We felt secure as he had food, which we didn't have, in the event we became stuck again. We were driving along with the driver looking out through his side window and I looking out through the passenger side window, both calling out when we could see the shoulder of the road or a ditch. Eventually, we became stuck and had to get out and put chains on the back wheels of the truck. That was no easy feat in the by now raging blizzard, but we managed to get it done and continued on our way once again.

After a while, we missed the side of the road and drove the truck into a ditch. There was no way to get it out without a tow truck, and that was not likely to happen in such a terrible snowstorm. We had a three-person discussion, and as we did not have enough gas to keep the engine running for a prolonged time, we were persuaded by the truck driver that he knew where we were and that we could walk to the nearest settlement of Eddy's Cove. We were all well-dressed for the weather as Gerry, and I had been snowmobiling in the Gros Morne Park a few days before and had our winter gear, including goggles, good gloves, hat, and scarves, which we felt confident would keep us warm.

We continued to make another doubtful decision and agreed to start walking the distance to Eddy's Cove. After about two hours of walking, if you could call it that, we stopped and discussed whether to dig a snow hut and settle in for the night or to continue on. At this stage, it was difficult to know if we were still walking on the roadway or through the barrens. We decided to carry on, and after about another hour and a half, we spotted a dim light blinking in the distance. Our spirits became buoyed, and we headed for the light, which was the first house in Eddy's Cove. It was now about 1:00 a.m., and we approached the house and knocked on the door. It was promptly opened, and we were greeted and asked in. We were told that we were probably the men that the Mounties had sent out word to see if anybody had seen us, as the Department of Highways Official had advised them. We had left St. Anthony in the morning, and their equipment operators were not able to locate us.

The house was small, and there were no spare beds for us to use. However, the lady of the home made us lunch and got us a hot cup of tea and some toast, which we all devoured. We were told that the Department of Highways still had a grader on the road looking for us, and it was expected to be passing by this home in a half hour. I negotiated with one of the boys in the house to rent his pickup truck for fifty dollars with an agreement that I would leave it at Flowers Cove for him the next day. We went up to the roadside and waited until the snowplough came along and stopped. The driver asked if we were the people they were looking for, and when I confirmed we were, he was happy and said he would report us safe and continue on his way.

I told him that as he was going on toward the south, we would follow him in our pickup truck. He was not happy with this, but reluctantly agreed. The grader could only drive a few miles per hour, as the visibility was too poor to see where the road surface was. Numerous times he had to stop and replough to find where the road was. After a half hour, the grader stopped, and the driver came back and told me he had received a call advising him that there was a medical emergency in the next community, and we were to stop there and pick up the patient and try to get her to the Flowers Cove Medical clinic.

This was sort of good news to me, as it meant we were going to get as far as Flowers Cove that night. We drove along with the wind and snow raging and, after a while, came upon a car with a few people around it. We stopped and were told that the lady was pregnant and had developed complications, and the doctor advised to try to get her to the medical clinic as soon as possible. There were a number of further complications. The grader operator advised he did not have enough gas to go the distance to Flowers Cove, and he relayed this to his supervisors. They then arranged for a front-end loader, which was in a community further south, to leave and meet us along the way. We would then transfer the patient from the grader to the loader. The operator said that it would not be comfortable for the patient in the tractor, so it was decided she would come with us in the pickup truck. This was good news to me, as by now, the tractor operator was glad were along with him on this journey, and we were more likely to get all the way to Flowers Cove.

We continued along, eventually meeting the front-end loader, which relieved the grader operator. Then the front-end loader commenced escorting us to Flowers Cove. We arrived in Flowers Cove at 5:00 a.m. and took the lady to the clinic, and then we went up the street to the local motel. We were hoping they would have a spare room, but in any event, they could at least take us in from the cold until we decided what to do. There was a snowdrift completely up to the top of the front motel door. We found a shovel and shoveled away enough snow for the door to open, and we knocked on the door. A man wearing a pair of pants and long johns answered and invited us in. When I inquired if he had any vacant rooms, he said we could have the whole motel as there were no other guests there.

We checked in and, being exhausted, immediately went to bed. We slept for a few hours, and I awakened to the aroma of food cooking in the dining room. I called Gerry, and we got dressed and went to the dining room for something to eat. We were hungry as the only meal we had the day before was the lunch served in our hosts' home at Eddy's Cove. When the lady, owner, and head cook came out to take our order, I told her that what we smelled seemed to be incredibly good and asked if she could tell us what it was and if we could probably have some. She advised it was salt fish that she had cooked for her husband, but she did not think we would like it and that she and her husband had eaten all that she had cooked.

There weren't many options on the menu, but we both ordered cold roast beef sandwiches. When the sandwich came, I tried to eat it, but the meat was hard. I checked under the slice of bread and saw that the roast beef was rather black, dry, and tough. I wasn't sure about eating it and decided against it. The lady came over and asked if anything was wrong, and I told her we really weren't that hungry and if she could just make us a couple of slices of toast. We eventually enjoyed our breakfast and plotted what we were going to do. The forecast was for the storm to continue for another day. It had already completely closed the highway, and it was not expected to open until the next day. I called the highways depot at Plum Point and inquired if they had any equipment on the road that could come toward Flowers Cove and escort us further south. The storm was not as severe down around Parsons Pond and on south, so if we could make it there, we could carry on to Deer Lake and get a flight home to St. John's.

In the meantime, I received a call that evening before retiring from an RCMP officer who advised he was at Flowers Cove and was anxious to get back to Corner Brook. He heard that we were going to be escorted by the highways plough when conditions permitted and asked if he could come along. This was great news to me, as I readily agreed on condition he take me and my colleague along since we did not have any transportation. He was happy with this arrangement, and I agreed we would have the plough operator swing by the RCMP depot and clear out his car and then come to the motel and pick us up.

The highways depot officials had advised me the weather was too bad to put the equipment on the road, but as soon as he could dispatch a tractor to the area, he would contact me to arrange for us to follow the plough south once it arrived in our area.

It looked like we were going to be at the motel for another day, so I asked the owner if he had a bottle of rum we could purchase from him so we could read and have a drink or two. He said he could give us a drink but that was all he had. Well, I thought for a while and then decided to call the welfare officer and ask if she had any books we could borrow as we didn't have any reading material with us, having left all of our baggage in the grocery truck somewhere in a ditch on the Northern Peninsula. She said yes, and I agreed to get dressed and walk over to her home. When we arrived there, she had lots of books, and I asked if she might have a bottle of wine or rum we could purchase. She did not, but she agreed to call the local liquor store manager, and he agreed to go to meet us at the store and let us in to make a purchase.

We returned to the motel, and around suppertime, I again phoned the highways depot for a progress report and was told that it didn't look promising for getting equipment on the road that night, and he would reassess in the morning and let me know. I wasn't convinced that I was getting much sympathy from the depot officials, and they may not try to rescue me when they could. I decided to call the deputy minister of transportation, who was a friend of mine, in St. John's and advise him of our plight and enlist his support to ensure that the local highways depot officials would help us out when they could. He assured me of his support, and later that evening, I got a telephone call from the depot advising me that they would have a tractor on the road early in the morning, and they would be in my area around 7:00 a.m. That was good news, so I called the RCMP officer and advised him, and we settled into a good book and retired early to be up and dressed when the tractor arrived in the morning.

Later that night, I received a call from the RCMP officer advising that he had just been notified of the death of a man in Plumb Point, and he was to stop there to collect the body and take it to Corner Brook with him for an autopsy. He said we could not go there right away, as the family needed some time to have a wake and mourn before he took the body away. I could not believe what I was hearing—what else could go wrong? Well, I had no choice but to agree with him, and I called the highways depot to ask them to hold off on sending the tractor to Flowers Cove for us. They were glad to do so for two reasons: one the weather was still blowing considerably, making visibility extremely poor, and the other was that the man who died was one of their supervisors, and they wanted to cooperate with the family to whatever extent they could. We agreed that they would change the schedule and arrange to arrive in Flowers Cove around noon.

We were fully dressed and waiting for the sound of the tractor when, finally, I heard it and watched as it passed by the motel toward the RCMP station. We patiently waited for it to return as the RCMP station was only a short distance past the motel. A long time passed, and the tractor did not return, so we decided to walk up the road to the RCMP station to see what was causing the delay. We walked a short distance and spotted the grader stopped in the middle of the road. When we arrived there, the operator advised me that the wheel had fallen off the tractor and he could not go any further. He had contacted his depot, and they had dispatched another front-end loader, and it would arrive in about two hours' time.

Finally, the front-end loader arrived, dug out the RCMP cruiser, and we were on our way following the loader as close as we could before the snowdrifts would block our way. I was now wondering how we were going to manage a dead body in the car with the three of us. The sergeant advised me he had a body bag in the trunk, and we would put the body in it and carry it in the trunk. I was somewhat comforted by this, as I had an uneasy feeling about driving with the body in the back seat.

When we arrived in Plumb Point, we first went into the local motel for a slice of toast and a cup of coffee. While there, the motel owner came over to chat, and upon discovering what our mission was, he offered to take the body in his pickup truck to Corner Brook for us. The RCMP sergeant agreed to pay his expenses, and we were greatly relieved that we would not have to deal with the dead body in our car.

We went to the home of the deceased person. It was situated in a field some distance from the road and covered in about two feet of snow. We made our way to it and knocked on the door. We were greeted by a member of the grieving family, and when the sergeant introduced himself and advised we were there to take the body for an autopsy, we were invited in.

The Mountie advised the family that we would wait until they finished their prayers, and we would then take the body from the home. When they finished, we were told to go into the kitchen where the body was. We were pleasantly surprised that the body was sitting on the kitchen table in a casket. We asked the family to leave the room and proceeded to close the cover on the casket only to find that as the deceased was a rather large gentleman and the cover would not close. After some cajoling, we managed to get it closed and clipped shut.

The kitchen was small with a lit stove near the kitchen door. We went to take the casket out of the kitchen but could not make the turn into the hall without standing the casket on its end. We had a short conversation to be sure we tipped it with the feet at the bottom and maneuvered it out the hall and out the front door. We put it on a bobsled and pulled it to the road and placed it into the truck and departed for Deer Lake and Corner Brook.

I stopped in at Cow Head to use the phone and called the Government Air Services and luckily found that the Government King Air was en route to Deer Lake with a cabinet minister and would be immediately returning to St. John's. I arranged to catch and board it while it was in Deer Lake, which was fortunate as there were no other commercial flights from Deer Lake to St. John's that day.

It was one of the happiest moments of my life when I arrived home exhausted and looking scraggly, not having shaved for the entire three days. The next day, I had to track down our luggage, which was in the truck in the ditch on the Northern Peninsula, and to retrieve the rental car that I had rented and had abandoned in a ditch somewhere between St. Anthony and Eddy's Cove. I was able to track down the truck driver, and he had already retrieved his truck and had our baggage at his home in Flowers Cove. I arranged for a colleague of mine who was working in Rocky Harbour to go to Flowers Cove and get our baggage and to continue along the highway and try to find the rented car. He called me that night to advise that he had my baggage and luckily had located the car, although he said it was barely visible from the road. He arranged for a tow truck to meet him the next morning and tow the car back onto the road and return it to the rental agency in Deer Lake.

The next summer, I met the deputy minister of highways, and I was thanking him for his assistance and the cooperation of his staff in the St. Barbe Depot. He started to laugh and told me that when he visited his depots in Plum Point and St. Anthony, they both told him about these two guys from St. John's who got stuck on the Northern

Peninsula and thought they could carry on as if it were the middle of the summer. Well, I guess they had a good laugh, and after we got over the exhaustion and had our luggage and the rental car returned, we also had a good laugh. It was a memorable trip, but if I hadn't been there, I would never have believed that those series of events could have happened.

The Travel Claim

Most of my career jobs required me to travel extensively throughout Newfoundland and Labrador, but when I was in middle management, the travel allowance for meals was very meager. The allowance for three meals would only cover the cost of one reasonable dinner at the end of the day. Inevitably, I would have to subsidize my own travel if I were to have breakfast and lunch. The government regulations did allow for reimbursement of meals based on actual receipts, but most often, I would forget to get a receipt so claiming the per diem was the easiest thing to do.

However, on one occasion, I was traveling with the assistant deputy minister of the department, and at the end of the day, we ended up at Ackerman's Hotel in Glovertown for the night. We agreed to meet for dinner in the dining room. I was there at the prescribed time, and in a few minutes, my assistant deputy minister arrived. After looking over the menu, he said he was going to order a steak. My travel allowance would not cover the cost of a steak, so I never ordered one when I was on the road. However, as my boss was having it, I thought I would do the same.

We had a lovely meal and a great chat, and when the bill came, I asked for a receipt to see if I could get reimbursed for it when I filed my travel claim. My chief accountant had to approve all travel claims. He never traveled and had a funny view of anyone that did. He thought anyone that traveled was on the road having a good time and they only deserved the minimum meal allowance.

The fourteen-dollar steak dinner was more than the full day's meal allowance, but I decided to claim it as I felt that if my boss could claim it, then I should be able to do the same when I was with him. I submitted my travel claim to the chief accountant, and after a few days, it had not been returned to me as was the usual practice.

Normally it would be approved and returned for payment in one or two days. I waited a few more days and then decided to go see the accountant to see if he had mislaid my claim.

When I asked him about it, he said, "No, I have it here, and I wanted to speak to you about it." He advised that he was not prepared to authorize the payment of that much for dinner, as he didn't want to set a precedent for other employees. I explained the circumstances to him, and he advised he was not going to change his mind. I was terribly upset and asked him to give me back my travel claim, and I would decide what to do about it. In fact, I already knew what I was going to do with it. He said the "what to do was simple"—just change to the per diem rate, and it would be processed.

I quickly took the claim, and without returning to my office, I went directly to the office of the assistant deputy minister and asked his secretary if I could see him. She sensed some anxiety and said he was free, and she would check with him to see if it was OK for me to go in. He immediately said yes, and when I went in, I passed him my travel claim and advised him that the chief accountant would not approve it as I was claiming for a steak dinner, and he thought it was exorbitant. Without asking a question and while we were still talking, he had signed the approval, and I thanked him and left.

I immediately brought the claim to the chief accountant and passed it to him and advised him I needed it paid within a few days, as I had been scheduled to travel again next week. He had no choice but to take it and have it processed for payment. After that, I always took my travel claims to the assistant deputy minister for approval before presenting them to the chief accountant for payment.

This was just one case of what I considered to be a small-minded individual asserting his own authority without any understanding of the circumstances or any appreciation of human relations skills in dealing with and managing a group of employees. Also, every now and then, I would deliberately save all my meal receipts and made sure they exceeded the meager government per diem allowance and have it approved for payment so I could tease the chief accountant.

Jumping Out of a Helicopter:

During my tenure as assistant deputy minister in the Department of Municipal and Provincial Affairs, I was responsible for the emergency services divisions, which included the Emergency Measures Organization and the Office of the Fire Commissioner. I had not been involved in this sector before, so I decided to attend a few training sessions to get a good understanding of their function and responsibilities.

The Emergency Measures Organization had a volunteer ice blasting team, which was used to explode ice jams that threatened to flood nearby communities in the spring each year. They had a team of specialists who made IEDs (dynamite bombs), transported them to the site, drilled holes in the ice, planted the sticks of dynamite, and created a planned blast that would break up the solid ice.

These people had a very demanding job that required them to practice hard to maintain the utmost safety in a very dangerous activity.

I attended a winter training exercise on a lake in central Newfoundland where the team would conduct their training. They used a helicopter with the doors removed to transport them and their explosives from shore to a position in the river where the ice jam had formed. They would have to rappel down a line from the helicopter and stand on the ice still tethered to the chopper for safety reasons and drill the holes in the ice and carefully plant their dynamite bombs. They would then be lifted, still hanging from their ropes from the chopper, to the safety on the shoreline from where they would explode the dynamite they had planted. As I was watching this routine being repeated several times with different team members, one of the members approached me and asked if I would like to try rappelling from the chopper. I knew that I had been ambushed by the team to see if I had the courage do it. Even the director, who was female, had gone through the procedure as part of the team. I knew I had no choice but to say yes and give it a try.

The supervisor began to brief me and put on my safety harness. The director advised me that they had two safety officers, one on the ground and one in the helicopter. The person on the ground could control your rate of descent from the helicopter and stop you completely if necessary. I was shown how to hold the single line that you rappelled on and how to control your rate of descent by applying thumb pressure on the line. I was warned not to go too fast, as I would burn through my gloves on the rope. It all seemed so simple.

Then I got into the helicopter, and we lifted off to several hundred feet. I suspected they brought me a bit higher for impact. I was not sure what the helicopter safety officer's job was, but he checked all my gear, harness connections, and gave me instructions. It was necessary to get out on the helicopter pontoon, and that is why the doors had been removed to facilitate this. I was then advised to lower my body over the pontoon and rappel to the ground. The safety officer advised me not to look down when I got out of the helicopter, as I may lose my nerve and not want to go.

When I got out onto the pontoon, I had to look to see how far I had to go, and I immediately realized the value of the safety officer's advice not to look down. I hesitated to try to decide what to do. It was at that moment that I found out the real job of the helicopter safety officer as I felt his size 12 boot against my back and heard him say "Goodbye, Mr. Peckham." I began to descend, ignoring the instruction to go slow, and I rapidly moved toward the ground when suddenly, I stopped in midair. I thought I must have snagged the line, but I could not figure that out as there was only a single line from which to rappel. Then I began to slowly descend and safely reached the ground. The safety officer came over and asked to see my hands. My leather gloves had completely burned through, and if it weren't for his quick work in stopping my descent when he did, I would have severely burned my hands.

It was a great experience, and I did it a second time with much more success than the first time. I certainly learned of the dangerous tasks the team had to perform and the demanding training they undertook to keep them sharp at their skills.

Fire Training Exercise

On another occasion, I was invited by the fire commissioner to attend a firefighters training exercise being held at one of the local fire training facilities on the Southern Shore. The commissioner was a dedicated professional and always took an opportunity to show off the several thousand volunteer firefighters training requirements and their skills. These volunteers are an extremely dedicated group of people. They must attend training school to acquire various levels of firefighting efficiency and then continue to practice at their local fire hall to hone their skills and be ready to meet the call when a fire emergency occurs in their town.

I drove up the Southern Shore to the training facility and was greeted by the fire commissioner, the local fire chief, and the training candidates. Today they were practicing going through smoke- and fire-filled buildings and searching in the blazing inferno for fire victims trapped inside.

The training building was full ablaze, and a number of firefighters with full firefighting equipment and breathing apparatus were receiving their last-minute instructions. They each teamed up with a buddy. Buddies are to look out for each other in this hugely dangerous situation as they had to enter the blazing inferno. They were told that there would be victims (planted training dummies) they were to locate and bring out.

After a number of rounds, the fire chief asked if I wanted to dress up and go through to experience what the firefighters had to endure. I agreed, and two members started to suit me up and explain what each piece was for and how it would protect me in the extreme heat of the live fire. By the time he loaded the breathing apparatus on my back, I was barely able to stand up under the weight of all the protective clothing and the breathing apparatus.

An experienced firefighter was assigned to lead me and another to follow. I am sure the fire commissioner and chief did not want anything to happen to a senior bureaucrat that they would have to answer for. I was given instructions on how to proceed and to maintain contact with my lead and search for victims while crawling through the first and second levels of the fire house. The going was tough; there was a tremendous amount of heat and almost zero visibility. I didn't find any victims on the first level and was apprehensive about going up stairs in such a blazing inferno darkened by extreme smoke, thinking that I would have to come back through it all again to get out.

We reached the second level, and in the hallway, I felt the shape of a person. I felt good that I was able to find one of their plants and get to carry it with me to an open window and pass it out to a fellow firefighter who would take it down the ladder to safety. When I tried to lift it, I realized it was too heavy for me to pick up with all the gear it had on. I motioned to my lead firefighter, and he came to my rescue only to find out that the victim we had found was a real firefighter. The victim was a firefighter trainer who was in the building and had overstayed his available air source and had been overcome by the lack of oxygen.

He was lifted by both of us to the window and passed out to the waiting firefighter who, needless to say, was surprised that we were handing him off a live firefighter that we had just rescued.

I certainly learned how difficult a firefighter's job can be and the dangers they place themselves in each and every time they respond to a call. My respect for them grew immensely after having an opportunity to get a taste of what they go through.

Dealing with the Mafia

You would never think that working in the public service would require you to work with a mafia figure, but it happened to me.

The government of the day embarked on a program of having new government buildings built on a lease/buy-back arrangement. This would require less initial financial outlay, and the government would not have to find all the money in one or two years to build these required facilities.

One of the buildings built under this plan was a college building, and when completed, it was put on a lease/buy-back arrangement with the owners guaranteeing the structure and exterior of the building and including the roof for a period of ten years. After a few years, the developers sold the building to another company, but it was subject to the same terms and conditions that existed between the previous owner and the government.

After a while, I would occasionally get a call from James Princeton, a principal in the new company, directing me to send their monthly payments to a specified bank account. This happened a few times with instructions for deposit into a different bank each time. This did not mean anything to me at the time, and we merely complied with the owner's request.

After about six or seven years into the buy-back arrangement, the roof of the building began to leak. I contacted the owner and requested that they undertake repairs to correct the problem. They did respond and did some remedial work, but did not do a complete roof replacement.

This cured the problem for about a year when new leaks developed. I contacted the owners and again requested them to make the required repairs, which they again agreed to do. However, time passed by and there was no sign of the owners correcting the problem.

This dragged on into the next year, and in addition to the leaking roof, the brick siding began to deteriorate and several sections had fallen away from the wall. I contacted the owners and advised them and demanded they take immediate corrective action to fix both the roof and the building sides. The owner did not respond, and time was passing by as we were now into the eight year of the warranty period. I wanted to make sure that the owners made all the required repairs before we reached the expiry date of the ten-year warranty.

When it became apparent that the owner was delaying the repairs and there was a possibility of us running the time limit on the warranty, I contacted our department lawyer in the Department of Justice and asked for legal advice on the best course of action to follow to ensure the owners met their warranty responsibilities.

One evening at home, I was watching a documentary on CBC television on the top mafia people in Canada. One of the people listed was the principal of the firm that owned the building we were leasing from, and he was the person with whom I had been dealing with throughout the term of the lease/buy-back agreement.

I advised the Department of Justice of this, and we were then more concerned that the owners would delay the repairs and try to run out the warranty period. The lawyers advised me that we should issue a legal notice to the developer of our intent to sue them in court to ensure they complied with the terms of the warranty provisions of the buy-back agreement.

We had considered holding back the monthly payments for the building, but there was a legal restriction in the lease/buy-back agreement prohibiting us from withholding rent for any reason, so we had to proceed without this option available to us.

The Department of Justice prepared all the legal papers needed to start the court proceedings, and they were required to have the notice served personally on the owner of the building, Mr. James Princeton, the named mafia figure in the CBC exposure.

I telephoned his headquarters to find out when he would be in his office, which was in California, but was never able to get any information from his receptionist and never able to get through to him.

The Department of Justice agreed to pursue finding this gentleman and to arrange to have the papers served on him. I went on vacation to Florida for a well-deserved break. While there, I received a phone call from the solicitor in the Department of Justice, and he advised me that he had tracked down Mr. Princeton and he was at one of his offices in Miami.

He felt that as I was already in Florida, I would be the best person to bring the legal papers to Mr. Princeton and serve them personally on him. I was a bit leery of doing this, but when I thought about it, I really didn't have any choice but to take a few days from my vacation in Florida and drive over to Miami and see if I could locate Mr. Princeton.

Our solicitor arranged to courier me the legal papers overnight, and the next day, I set out for Miami, not to enjoy it as one would wish, but to find the elusive Mr. Princeton and serve him with the papers.

I went to the Miami address that I was given, and it was indeed an impressive office building. I went up to the second floor where this firm was located and hesitatingly went in the front entrance. There was an open reception area, very well finished in hardwood and a plush carpet with leather sofa and chairs.

I approached the receptionists and asked if I could see Mr. Princeton. She wanted to know the reason for my visit as I did not have an appointment. I was wondering how to respond when a gentleman came out of a nearby office and asked what I wanted. The receptionist referred to him as Mr. Princeton when advising that I was here to see him, but I did not have an appointment.

I now knew I had the correct person, and I immediately seized on the chance and told him that I had a message to deliver to him in person. I passed him the envelope and, he reached over and accepted it. I did not tell him my name, and even though we had spoken on the phone on numerous occasions, we had never met in person. I advised him that this was a legal summons, and I confirmed that I had personally delivered it to him.

I departed the office with great relief and proceeded back to Florida where my family was waiting for me to finish my vacation. I phoned our solicitor in the Department of Justice and advised him I had successfully served the summons. He was delighted and somewhat surprised that I was able to get this done in such short order.

Eventually, Mr. Princeton telephoned me to advise that they intended to completely replace the roof on the building and to replace and repair the exterior walls as required. Over the next summer, this work was undertaken and completed to the satisfaction of our departmental engineers.

We did not have any problem with the roof or walls after that. So much for working in a safe civil service job!

Like a Dog after a Bone

As a senior public servant responsible for finance and administration in the Department of Public Works and Services, I would invariably have to accompany the minister in attendances before the government's Public Accounts Committee.

These were unique experiences. The job of the committee, which was made up of members from the government and the opposition, but always with a government majority, was to examine the department's estimates and question the minister and his/her senior officials on the reason for various expenditures and to make sure that the government only spent the money for the purpose for which it was approved.

The opposition members used this opportunity to try and embarrass the minister by prying into expenditures that they thought were wasteful or inappropriately used. Of course, most ministers would defer to their senior finance person to answer the detailed questions.

On one occasion, I was attending a committee meeting with the minister. Steve Neary, an opposition member, began questioning the minister about a lease that the government had entered into with the owners of Atlantic Place on Water Street for some office space. The PC opposition knew that the property was owned by a prominent liberal and wanted to make it look to the public like it was a sweetheart deal between government and its friends.

I was not only responsible for managing the finances for the department, but I was also responsible for the Government Purchasing Agency, which would handle tenders for the purchase of goods and services for all government departments. In this case, the agency called for proposals on behalf of our department for office space in the St. John's area, and after evaluation, the Atlantic Place bid was the lowest one that met the criteria of the proposal call.

At the hearings, when the minister was briefly asked for information on the lease arrangement, he suggested to the committee chairman that I was the best person to question as the lease arrangement came under my responsibility in the department.

This was agreed to, and I was called to be questioned. I provided all the information on the lease, such as the price, the size of the space leased, and the general terms and conditions.

The opposition member, Mr. Steve Neary, kept probing me to try to get me to name the individual that owned the property, which he knew very well, but I kept responding that we did not lease the property from an individual, but rather from a corporation, and I gave him the name of the owner, St. John's Development Corporation, which was public information anyway.

Mr. Neary was determined to get me to name the owner of the corporation, but I was not prepared to get baited into his ploy to be the person to name the shareholders of the corporation. I did not want to get caught in his political gamesmanship with our minister and normally a member of the House of Assembly would not put a public servant in such a position. Mr. Neary could easily find the owner of the corporation by checking with the Registry of Companies, but he wanted to connect it to this lease arrangement and make it sound politically motivated.

Normally I would be questioned for thirty or forty minutes on this type of activity, but Mr. Neary wouldn't give up, and he continued to badger me and asked questions over and over and return to who is the owner of the property. When I continued to tell him that it was the St. John's Development Corporation, he continued to say yes, but who owns that. I told him we didn't deal with individual shareholders of the corporation, but with its business representatives.

He got frustrated and said, "You would probably deal with the mafia," to which I replied, "Sir, I wouldn't know the difference." This got him more irritated, and he was determined to punish me by continuing to question me on the subject. The chairman called a recess, and while I was pouring myself a coffee, a prominent minister of the government came over to me and whispered in my ear that Steve was like a dog chasing a bone but wasn't sure what he should do with it.

After recess, the questioning continued, and Mr. Neary continued his questioning for almost two full days before finally giving up. I still often get a chuckle when I think of this from time to time. Usually as a public servant, you would try not to get members of the house of assembly mad with you, and I always made a point of dealing with members from the House of Assembly equally and as fairly as I could. But in this case, Mr. Neary pushed me, and I decided to push back a bit, but unfortunately for me, he didn't see the humor in my response.

CHAPTER 10
WORKING IN THE POLITICAL ENVIRONMENT

The Political Environment

Working in the political environment was a unique and most interesting experience. I had the unique perspective of seeing its operations from the time I started out at age eighteen working in the public service as a junior clerk in the Audio-Visual Division of the Department of Education to working my way up through the ranks to eventually become a director and, later, as an assistant deputy minister of two separate departments.

I spent thirty-nine years working in the public service and, for a good part of that time, at a senior and executive level. This had me working closely with literally hundreds of politicians and their political staff. It made for a most interesting time as there were some first-rate gentlemen and ladies, some were experienced and knew how to deal with the bureaucrats effectively and decently, while a few were plainly incompetent and ignorant. I have selected just a few of the memorable incidents from ministers who were great to work with, and some who were simply incompetent, sometimes arrogant due to their insecurity and did not trust their senior staff. I worked with a lot of ministers as I worked with every government from 1959 to 1996. In all, I had worked for six premiers: Joseph R. Smallwood, 1959–1972; Frank D. Moores, 1972–1979; Brian Peckford, 1979–1989; Thomas Rideout, March 1989–May 1989; Clyde Wells, 1989–1996, and Brian Tobin, 1989–1996.

The following are my perspective on a few.

Can You Offer Him More Money?

One day while working in my office, my boss called me and said that the premier Hon. Joseph Smallwood wanted to see me. I went to his office on the tenth floor of the Confederation Building and was eventually escorted into his office, the premier was obviously annoyed at something, and this soon became evident. He became annoyed with me for not offering more money to a resident whose property had been expropriated for a public works activity. While I was explaining that I had the property professionally appraised and I had offered the full value plus 10 percent, the premier kept jumping up and down, demanding to know who had approved my offer. The offer had been approved by my deputy minister, whom I knew was also a personal friend of the premier. I did not want to name him, so I kept saying "The deputy minister," all the while, the Premier, by now quiet red-faced, kept jumping up and down screaming, "Who, who, who!" When I finally named the deputy, he settled down and immediately dismissed me from his office.

The next time I heard about this offer was from my boss, who asked if there was any way we could increase the offer. I told him that we could not reasonably do so, but I could consider a relatively small adjustment for injurious affection, and this was agreed to, and the offer was slightly increased and soon after accepted by the property owner. It wasn't long after that I heard that the property owner in question was going to run for politics, which he did, and I then realized how he had gotten the premier to intervene in the negotiations for his property on his behalf.

Unique Financing

When I was the director of expropriations, I was often scrambling to acquire property in a hurry as the government inevitably would enter into agreements for some form of economic development that required them to purchase land for the development. However, most of these development agreements were kept private until they were completed, and the government could make a public announcement. Only after that was I advised that property was required, and then it had to be bought quickly, as the developer would want to start immediate construction.

In addition to the tight scheduling problem, I had to deal with more often than not there would not be any money in the current year's budget to pay for the required property. To deal with these cases, the premier of the day had set up a three-person finance committee. These were three prominent senior civil servants, and they were given the authority to arrange interim financing for projects that had not been budgeted for.

When I needed money to conclude a purchase arrangement, I would let the special finance committee know, and in a few days or so, they would advise me of the financing arrangement.

On one occasion, I had concluded a purchase agreement with the Anglican Diocesan Synod to buy the Anglican orphanage on Prince Philip Parkway, which was needed to build the new Arts and Culture Centre. There was no money in the budget for this project, so I contacted the chairman of the special finance committee and advised him that I needed over a million dollars to close the deal. Within a few days, I was advised that arrangements had been made with Lundrigan's Limited to provide the interim financing. I contacted the principal of the company, and he confirmed that the financing had been arranged. He agreed to send the company commander airplane in to St. John's to pick me up take me to Corner Brook to get the check. I did this, picked up a check for over a million dollars, flew back to St. John's, delivered the check to the solicitor for the Diocesan Synod, and concluded the purchase agreement.

The next budget had provision for the cost of the property, and I could then arrange to have the amount borrowed from Lundrigan's Limited repaid to them.

Can You Hear Me, Detective?

Premier Smallwood had an electronic communications system between his office and the offices of all his ministers and deputy ministers. The premier could call directly to either minister or deputy to question them or to summon them to his office. In addition, he could activate the system and listen in on any conversation taking place in any of those offices. Because of this, most ministers and deputies learned to be cautious as to what they would say when they were in their office.

The following premier, Frank Moores, had the system removed, but the minister Hon. Bill Doody, whom I worked for at the time, didn't trust the security within his office and always started off his comments by looking at the ceiling and saying, "Can you hear me, Detective?" I am not sure if he had good reason to suspect there was snooping or if it was just his cautious nature. In any event, we would always carefully choose our words in his office. That minister had a great sense of humor, and it was always a pleasure to travel with him. While doing business he was always a consummate professional and in our off time he could keep us in stitches with laughter with his hilarious stories.

I Am Fired

Another minister I worked with, the Honorable Haig Young, was a fine gentleman and also had a great sense of humor; unfortunately, he often drank too much liquor and then his personality changed into a mistrusting and mean character. It was probably caused by his lack of self-confidence in his ability. He was fond of listening to his constituents when he was home on the weekends and would take what he heard as being the gospel truth without questioning it or checking the facts. He would inevitably come into the office Monday mornings and have one or two staff names and demand they be fired. When I would question him, he would become uneasy and tell me what he heard about the person. Most of the time, he was hearing from some of his constituents that were hired as temporary staff and who felt that because the minister hired them, they didn't have to work very hard or hardly work at all. Of course, their supervisors didn't treat them any different than any other worker and demanded a decent day's work effort. They resented this and would tell the minister their supervisor was incompetent or something to that effect, and the Honorable Haig Young would think that was the gospel truth and demand that I discipline them.

I spent many of my Monday mornings defending staff from what I knew were ridiculous allegations without any substance whatsoever. The staff in question never knew they were being so maligned. On other occasions, Minister Young would be at a staff party and, after consuming a few drinks, would tell staff that he for some reason didn't like them and that they were fired. These would be career people with very credible records. I spent many hours counseling staff not to worry about being fired and to come in to work the next day. Nevertheless, the minister ruined Christmas for three staff persons when he told them they were fired at the staff Christmas party to which he had been invited as a guest. While I told those people not to worry, I know they went home with a lot of hurt in their heart for their Christmas holiday.

One of the "fired staff," a senior professional engineer, told me that he was going to go over and punch the minister, at which time I advised him, "Right now you are not fired, but if you punch the minister, you will then be fired." Luckily, he held off and went home. All returned to work after Christmas and carried on, and the minister likely didn't even remember what he had done.

Myself and my colleague, another assistant deputy minister, had been on the receiving end of the firing many times. My colleague told me that he had been fired four times the same day. On one occasion, in my case, we were at a public session with all the senior departmental staff for a staff training conference, and the minister got miffed with me because I invited the local judge to the suite and had offered him a drink. The minister was offended as he thought that he should have asked the honorable judge in for a drink himself even though he wasn't there at the time. This was a casual affair, and I had met the judge in the hotel corridor and extended our hospitality to him. Anyway, an hour or so into the reception, the honorable minister arrived and loudly proclaimed to the staff that I had been fired.

I left the reception and went to my room to relax as I was not worried that I was really fired. However, the staff was not used to this kind of behavior and were perplexed and didn't know just what to do. Many came and knocked on my door to offer me condolences, and I would advise each one not to worry; I would be at work tomorrow.

Our conference was due to start eight thirty next morning, and I was supposed to be the conference chairman, and the purpose for the minister's presence was to officially open the conference and tell the staff about the government's policy direction and programs.

I decided I had to let the staff know that I didn't do anything that would warrant me being fired. I knew that there was a good chance the minister would not make it to the meeting on time in the morning. So as the staff assembled, with me among them, we waited, and at the starting time when there was no minister, I decided not to convene the meeting but to wait. A half hour later, I sent a staff member to the minister's room to remind him that the staff were all waiting for him to arrive to start the conference. He advised the senior staff person to tell me to go ahead with the meeting and he would join us later on. I then called everyone into the meeting and advised them that I had been reinstated, and we would continue the business as usual. The minister sheepishly joined us at the lunch break.

This same minister hired many of his constituents in temporary and student jobs. It did not matter if they had any skills to do the work they were hired for, and often I thought that the reason they were hired was because they did not have any skills or capability. This made it very difficult for middle managers to manage their projects efficiently, for if they pushed the employees too hard, they would bring down the wrath of the minister on them and possibly be the next candidate to be "fired." These were the same people the honorable minister would listen to in the district on the weekends and come in convinced that some manager was not suitable for his job and he wanted him/her disciplined or fired.

The Fraud Case

When I was appointed assistant deputy minister of the Department of Public Works and Services, one of the first items I had to deal with was an ongoing fraud investigation. I had been assigned as the departmental coordinator to work with the police and the Department of Justice officials to facilitate the investigation. It was suspected that a local contractor had billed the government and was paid for a considerable amount of work that was never carried out and for materials that had not been used in the work. To do this, the contractor would have had to have the cooperation of an official working with the department.

Thousands and thousands of invoices had to be checked covering several years, and many jobs had to be inspected to see if the work had been carried out or not. It soon became evident that this would uncover a substantial fraud case in the range of hundreds of thousands of dollars. As the investigation progressed, we determined that the contractor had been given some confidential information from departmental files.

We had a departmental central registry that used a system of pinning notes onto file documents, and the files were logged out to employees. I checked our files and noticed that the document with the confidential information had two pin holes in it. This meant that the paper had been removed from the file and replaced. As the files had to be signed out to employees, I checked the log and identified the inspector that had borrowed this file. It turned out that this inspector was the same person that had certified all the invoices for the contractor stating the work had been completed and that the billed material had been used on the job.

This was pretty damning evidence against the employee, but we still did not have hard proof that he had taken the document out of the file. One day during the preliminary court hearings into this case, the inspector had been called to give evidence. I noticed that he had a file with papers in it that he referred to from time to time, and I suspected he might have a copy of the confidential document that went missing from our file.

When there was a break, I discussed this with our solicitor, and when court resumed, the solicitor asked the judge to have the inspector provide copies of the information in his file as he was using it in the proceedings. The judge agreed.

When the copies were passed over, there was a copy of the confidential document taken from the departmental files. This was enough evidence to directly connect the inspector to the contractor's fraud. He was caught red-handed.

The contractor was subsequently prosecuted and found guilty of defrauding the government of hundreds of thousands of dollars and was sentenced to time in jail. The inspector was dismissed from his job.

This case had consumed a considerable amount of my time, and it was a great relief when the trial was over so I could spend more time on managing the affairs of the department, as many of the accounting procedures were out of date and needed to be revised. I did this over the next several months, and we installed a new accounting system that contained appropriate checks and balances and allowed us to process invoices in a much timelier fashion.

Get the Contract Signed

Premier Honorable Frank Moores had agreed to engage a mainland consulting firm to do contract work for the government, and during budgeting time, the money for the contract was placed in the budget of my department. As I was responsible for finance and administration, I gathered all the information on the work the consultant was to do and headed off to their head office with a solicitor to negotiate a contract for the work. It was to be a fairly routine exercise, and I did not anticipate a problem until the vice president of the firm objected to having to provide receipts for expenditures they would incur during the contract. I told them we could not entertain a contract without full receipts for all expenditures, but the vice president was adamant in not wanting to do so. We were not able to conclude an agreement, so I headed back home.

The next day, when I went into my office, my boss asked me how come we did not reach an agreement with the consultant. I was surprised he knew, as I had not yet had a chance to brief him as to what had happened. He said had been told by the premier. I thought that odd and guessed that the consultant had a good connection with the premier's office.

A week later, I was told to go back to the consultant's office in Montreal to try to get a contract agreement, and I was advised that a senior official from the premier's office would accompany me. We went again to the head office of the company and spent the better part of two days discussing the contract conditions, but the submission of receipts became the sticking issue once again. I merely told all present that we were not ever going to have a contract if I could not get agreement to have receipts provided to support expenditures. So once again, there was a stalemate. The premier's staff person did not have any signing authority in my department and therefore was not in a position to influence the nature of the contract or to direct that it be signed without receiving receipts.

We went back to St. John's with the news we were not able to secure an agreement on contract terms, and therefore there was no contract in place. The contractor was putting pressure on my boss, and I suspect the premier's office, to get on with the work, but he was afraid to commence without a signed contract. A week later, the premier decided that the deputy minister, my boss, should go to the consultant's head office to see if he could resolve the issue and get a contract in place.

So we once again went to Montreal where we met again with the vice president of the company. My deputy minister asked me what we could do, and I advised him that we should do nothing unless they agreed to receipts or he overruled me and directly signed the contract, but I would neither sign nor recommend it.

Once the meeting started, my deputy got up and stated to the consulting firm's vice president that there was only one item keeping us from signing a contract, and it was the need to have receipts for expenditures incurred. He told the VP that there was nothing further he could do unless the consultant agreed to that provision. The vice president then stated that if that is the case, he would agree to the provision, and later that day, we each signed the contract, and the work was eventually carried out and properly accounted for.

I was curious to know how the premier knew all the details of my meetings in Montreal before I had a chance to return and advise my deputy minister. Later, I found out that the lady I was negotiating with was a girlfriend of the premier; in fact, he later married her.

It was ironic the next year when the auditor general was auditing our department, they asked to see a copy of the contract between the government and the consulting firm, which they reviewed in detail and stated they were satisfied that we had an excellent contract in place. I can only imagine the chaos that would have been created if they discovered that the contract didn't require the support of receipts for expenditures incurred on that job.

I Am Hired

From time to time, I would receive representation from ministers asking if a constituent of theirs could be considered for a job position that was available. On one such occasion, I advised the minister to have the person phone me and arrange an appointment, at which time I would determine his suitability for consideration to be given an interview for the job. The gentleman phoned, and I gave him a time to come and see me.

When he arrived in my office and I started to ask him what his qualifications and experience, he interrupted me and asked why I wanted to know all of that. I advised him that I needed to know to see if he was suitable to be granted a formal interview for the job. He immediately shouted at me to not waste my time, as he had already been given the job by one of the ministers. I advised him that was not so and again tried to explain to him the hiring process, but he would not let me continue as he continued to interrupt me and shout at me, telling me he had the job, and if I didn't cooperate, I would be out of a job. I then told him in a very stern voice to "Get out of my office" and "You will not be hired."

As he left, I telephoned the minister to advise him of what had happened before Sam got to him and told him his version. The minister said, "Don, I was afraid something like that was going to happen, and I will deal with Sam." That was the last I heard from that gentleman.

How to Evaluate Art

For several years, I was chairman of the Newfoundland Government Art Procurement Program, and the committee's deliberations had many amusing stories. I can say up front that I did not have any formal training in art, but the committee had two professional artists on its membership. My role was one of administration, although I did have a say in which pieces of artwork were to be purchased.

One day, I was looking over the art assembled for viewing by our committee, and there were many types and styles of work. Themes ranged from landscape to abstract, and they were in watercolors, oils, sculptures, triptychs, etc. It was always difficult trying to ensure that a good blend of various types of art was purchased and that there was a good representation from well-established artists and new artists.

While looking at the works on the wall, I was approached by Dr. Cyril Poole, the principal of the Grenfell College in Corner Brook and a noted artist in his own right. He asked me if I knew how to evaluate art, especially abstract pieces that had to be in the eye of the beholder. I told him, "No, I just use my own experience and preferences."

He said, "Here is how to do it, especially if there are others present and you don't want to disclose whether you like it or not." He said, "Just stand in front of the work and stare at it for a few moments, then tip your head slightly to one side and look for a minute or so, turn it to the other side and afterwards exclaim 'That is very interesting.' You could say this whether you liked the work or not." So that was my lesson in how to evaluate a piece of artwork.

The Red Trench

One of my jobs while I was at the Department of Public Works and Services was chairman of the Government's Art Procurement Program. The program provided for the purchase of artwork from local artists on a yearly basis. There were two purposes of the program: one was to provide a bank of artwork to be used to decorate the government office buildings, and the second was to stimulate the production of local art and assist artist in the process.

There was a committee consisting of three people—two government officials and one person from the arts community. We had purchased a lot of artwork over several years. Everything from watercolors, oils, triptychs, collages, and sculptures. In addition, we would, from time-to-time, commission a specially created piece of work.

One such piece was a work commissioned to a prominent artist Don Wright. He was to create a large mural that could be hung in the breezeway connecting the two government buildings at the Confederation Building complex. Don made a maquette (model) of the work for us to review. He did this and explained that the image represented him standing on the beach near his home in Admiral's Cove in his bare feet and making a V-shaped motion while the sea water ebbed in and out, creating this abstract image.

The committee was satisfied with the intent and gave the go-ahead for the creation. It was agreed that the artist would use his imagination in applying colors to the finished product. When it was finished, it was delivered to Confederation Building and installed in the corridor connecting the east and west block of the two government buildings.

It was huge in size, and as it turned out, it was a huge issue. Some women who viewed the work claimed that it was an obscene piece of work depicting a woman's vagina. One of these ladies was a prominent member in the premier's office and soon persuaded him of what they thought the image represented. This was leaked out to the press and soon became a public controversial topic.

Hon. Haig Young called me into his office to tell me that there was a lot of heat on the premier over that piece of work. I told the minister what the work supposedly represented, but I did agree that the artist took a little liberty in applying the colors, which gave it different interpretations depending on how one looked at it. I invited him to look at it with me to see what he thought. After viewing it, he said he thought it looked like a split cod fish with the sound bone exposed, and he did not find anything offensive in it.

The next day, the minister called me again and advised that the work was to be removed that evening after everybody had left the building. This was done, and the work was placed in storage.

After a few years had passed, the curator of the Arts and Culture Centre inquired about the piece and asked if she could display it at the Centre. This was agreed to, and she subsequently hung the work in that building. I did not hear any criticism of the work while it was displayed there, and it was later moved to Memorial University, where I suspect it still hangs today.

In the meantime, one day when I was attending a cocktail function, I was standing near a group of women and I could not help but hear that their conversation had to do with the Red Trench artwork. I decided to join them and one of them said to me that the artwork looked like a giant vagina and asked me to comment. I kept as straight a face as I could and replied, "I wouldn't know, ma'am, as I have never seen a giant vagina." This quickly ended that Red Trench discussion.

The Big Arse

The typical minister's office suite in a government building will contain a minister's office, a receptionist area, a boardroom where they can meet with visiting delegations, and a private washroom. One of the honorable gentlemen, Honorable Bossy O'Dell, whom I had the "pleasure" to work with, had a quirky and arrogant personality.

Hon. Bossy O'Dell was a rather large gentleman, and the toilet in his washroom was always getting clogged up. I continually had to call the Department of Public Works plumbers in to clear the problem. As it continued over a prolonged time, I decided to go over there when the plumbers arrived and see if I could find out why this problem continued to occur. I asked the plumber what the problem for this reoccurring could be, and with a straight face, he looked at me and said, "Mr. Peckham, what do you expect when you have an eight-inch arse shitting into a four-inch pipe?" Needless to say, I broke up laughing, but I could not come to tell the minister the obvious humor, as I did not want to incur any more of his vile on me or those staff members. But my colleagues and I often got a great laugh over this, as we thought of it from time to time.

The Wrong Kind of Minister

When I was working in the Department of Public Works and Services, I had an opportunity to attend some federal/provincial minister conferences as a support person for my minister. During that time, I met many people and became friends with some of them.

I had the pleasure to meet the Honorable Jim Garnier, a gentleman from Saskatchewan. He was from a large Mennonite family with eight or nine siblings. His dad had been a Mennonite clergy, and a number of his brothers became Mennonite ministers. His father was not particularly happy when he found out that Jim was not going to become a Mennonite minister and worse in his mind was that he was entering politics.

Jim got elected, and his party was in opposition for a few years, and his father did not know what to think of him. And then the premier called a general election, and Jim's party gained enough seats to form the government. The new leader, when forming his cabinet, invited Jim to become the minister of Works and Services, which Jim was delighted to accept.

He couldn't wait for the end of the day to rush home to tell his parents the good news. He arrived home late in the afternoon and went straight to his parents' home. He told his dad, "You will be so proud that I have become a minister just like you always wanted me to become." His dad just looked at him with a straight face and said, "Son, you missed the point—that is not the kind of minister I want you to be."

Red Notes from Minister

I worked for Minister Bossy O'Dell. He was a large person, arrogant and incompetent, such that the premier had to have him shadowed by another senior minister. He could not make a decision without having it approved by Minister Jonny Clifton. Bossy did not trust his senior staff and used to try to show his superiority by always "telling" us what was wrong instead of asking if something was wrong or needed to be corrected.

Most often nothing was wrong; he simply did not have the facts and would try to make sense of a situation without the benefit of the information supporting the issue. He had a habit of writing to me and my colleague, the other departmental assistant deputy minister, using "red ink" notes every Monday morning. I guess he wrote them over the weekend. They were usually nasty, arrogant, and sometimes insulting for their lack of facts-based opinions.

Most ministers would have regular meetings with the executive, and if they had any concerns, they would be discussed and properly dealt with. But this was not the case with Hon. Bossy O'Dell.

His practice of using red notes and his lack of trust concerned and disturbed me. My colleagues and I would often discuss how disgusting this practice was. I became offended to the point that I decided to respond to each and every note in the same red ink color and to provide an answer to the query or comment he had made. My colleague decided not to do this. After a while, I did not receive any more of these red ink notes, but my colleague continued to receive them right up to the time that Honorable Bossy O'Dell finally got defeated in a general election and therefore was no longer in the government.

Relationship between Minister and the Executive

I decided to save this topic for last, as I did not want it to take away from the humor of the preceding incidents. In my early days as an executive member of the government, I soon learned that there was a special trust between the minister and his/her executive team. Both could freely discuss issues with each other, and the minister would be given the best advice based on the experience and training of the executive member, and both would respect that advice. It did not mean that the minister would necessarily take the advice, as he also had to make political considerations, but at least he would have the benefit of the advice to consider along with his other inputs so he could make an informed and responsible decision.

I believe that the process best supported the minister and the government decision-making ability. However, I noticed over the years a distinct change in attitude by ministers toward their executive members. Many of the ministers seemed to become mistrustful of their executive and would not consult them on some policy issues. Therefore, some of the government decisions would be made based mostly on political considerations without proper regard for their economic cost or the workability of the policy or whether it had been tried before, etc.

It even went deeper than that with some ministers. I had received requests to exclude a certain official from some activity even though it was for something that was fully within his scope of responsibility. Another example would be when someone got recommended for a promotion and if the minister did not like that person, he would try to block the recommendation.

Having said that, I wish to state here that there were always ministers that very much respected the people working for them, and they developed a trusting and respectful bond. There were many very competent ministers from an administrative view, but here I am, talking about the few who had no idea how to manage an enterprise or group of people, and they did not seem capable or willing to do so.

I have not worked in the government sector now for a number of years, so I cannot attest to what the situation is today. However, I have frequent contact with senior government employees, and for the most, part they tell me that they can't wait until their retirement time comes so they can get out. I sense the morale is very low, and I do not see any employee program directed to fix the problem. If the morale problem is not corrected, the organization will not be efficient and the government will have a difficult time in recruiting and maintaining competent people to deliver its public services.

If the bond between the political side and the executive is not strong, government will make weak decisions based more on political considerations rather than weighing other economic and practical considerations, and therefore sometimes the policy will not work or will have to be modified at great expense to make them more effective.

Ministers need to build the special relationship with their executive team. This will allow them to get the best advice when needed and will put the executives in a better position to understand new government policy when it is made and to better direct its delivery.

In addition, the hiring authority extended to ministers for summer and temporary staff serves as an avenue to circumvent the merit system of the Public Service Commission, as those hired temporarily often are extended on and eventually made permanent. This dilutes the pool of qualified staff and weakens the quality of support to deliver in an efficient and effective manner government programs to the public.

My "Honorable" Art Reid Story

When I attained the age of fifty-five and had worked for some thirty-six years with the Newfoundland government, I had decided to soon retire. In April, I had been elected as the president of the Navy League of Canada, a volunteer position that would require two dedicated years of time to fulfil the position properly. Therefore, I thought that by September 1996, I would retire. However, I did not have the chance to voluntarily retire as I heard that the then premier Tobin had decided to get rid of all the executives in the government that were over fifty years old.

Sure enough, one Monday morning, the last week of March, I had been told by my deputy minister that he had received word that my job had been made redundant and I would be retired the first of April. Art Reid, the minister, did not have the guts to call me in and tell me himself. I was disappointed that this had happened without any discussion with me. During my last week at work, Art Reid avoided me; he didn't have the courage to speak with me, and he didn't even say thanks for my thirty-six years of service. In fact, I never received as much as a decent goodbye from anyone representing the government.

Premier Tobin retired a large number of people during the next six months. My boss, a respected deputy minister, who, like me, had made the public service his career, received a phone call at his home on a Sunday evening while he was having dinner with his family and was told that he didn't need not return to work the next day. What a despicable way to treat staff who had dedicated their lives to the public service.

Government lost a lot of its continuity by releasing so many senior staff in such a short time, and it cost the public treasury a considerable amount of money, as all those people had to be paid their redundancy and severance pay and would begin drawing on the pension fund before they would have done if they could have continued to work until they wished to retire. All the positions were subsequently filled, and therefore there was absolutely no savings to the government.

Minister Jonny Clifton Story

A part of my responsibilities as assistant deputy minister in the Department of Public Works and Services was the management of the Government Purchasing Agency. The agency was responsible to make all purchases of goods required by all departments of the government and some of the agencies. On major or sensitive cases, they would consult me, and my underlying principal was always get the best quality goods at the most competitive price and deliver the goods to the required department in time to meet their programming goals. The procurement officials had to be satisfied that the bidder could deliver the goods in accordance with these requirements.

Occasionally I would receive representation from a minister asking if special consideration could be given to a particular firm. I would always advise them that we had to consider the bid on the basis of the criteria outlined in the request for a quote, and it was necessary to evaluate all bids on the basis of price, giving priority to the best price, providing all the specifications of the bid were met. This satisfied most ministers; however, there were an occasional one that persisted in applying pressure to favor a particular supplier.

A very prominent minister, Honorable Jonny Clifton, known publicly as being most honest, with a "Mr. Clean" image, once called me to his office and requested that I disqualify a low bidder for a service that had been put out to tender. I advised him that the bid met all the criteria and that they had by far the lowest bid price. He then turned angry and advised me he would call in Honorable Haig Younge, who was my minister, which he did. He then demanded that the contract not be issued to the lowest bidder. He did not have a reason except, "the government didn't want that firm doing business with it." I repeated my stand and outlined for my minister's benefit the bidding policy and the fact that this bidder met all the criteria and were the lowest of those received. In addition, the firm had a good delivery record.

My minister did not pressure me further, and I was told that I could return to my office, which I did. I advised the director of the Purchasing Agency to proceed with the purchase to the most qualified bidder, which he did.

About a month later, I was told that Honorable Jonny Clifton had recommended to the premier that I be fired from my job. Fortunately for me, the premier did not feel strongly enough about the issue to have me terminated.

INDEX

CPSIA information can be obtained
at www.ICGtesting.com
Printed in the USA
BVHW030533080321
601859BV00001B/6

9 781698 705255